H O U S E H O L D

SOLUTIONS & SUBSTITUTIONS

EASY STRESS-REDUCING QUICK FIXES FOR THE

KITCHEN, BATHROOM, BEDROOM, LAUNDRY & STAINS, GARAGE & GARDEN

Dedicated to my mother, sister, husband and my four beautiful children (Austin, Kyah, Kristi and Jordan), for whom there are no substitutions.

REENA NERBAS

Household Solutions & Substitutions
by Reena Nerbas

First Printing – October 2005

Published by Publishing Solutions, a division of PrintWest Communications Ltd.

NOTICE: The solutions and substitutions described in this publication have not been tested by Publishing Solutions. Publishing Solutions gives no warranty as to the usefulness, or as to the safety, of the suggestions which follow. Any problems arising from the use of these solutions and substitutions are the responsibility of the user. Use of these recommendations is solely the decision of the reader. Every user assumes all risks of injury or damage to whatsoever kind which may result from the implementation of any and all suggestions herein. Readers are warned that the combination of solutions and substitutions involving the use of chemical agents may be dangerous.

Library and Archives Canada Cataloguing in Publication
Nerbas, Reena, 1967-

Household solutions & substitutions : easy stress-reducing quick fixes for kitchen, bathroom, laundry & stairs, garage and garden / Reena Nerbas ;
edited by Margo Embury

Includes index.

ISBN 1-897010-21-4

1. Home economics. 2. Do-it-yourself work–Micellanea.

I. Embury, Margo, 1943- II. Title. III. Title: Household solutions and substitutions

TX158.N47 2005 640 C2005-906327-0

Cover and page design by Brian Danchuk, Brian Danchuk Design, Regina

Book formatting by Iona Glabus

Designed, Printed and Produced in Canada by:
Centax Books, a Division of PrintWest Communications Ltd.
Publishing Director and Editor: Margo Embury
1150 Eighth Avenue, Regina, Saskatchewan, Canada S4R 1C9
(306) 525-2304 FAX: (306) 757-2439
centax@printwest.com www.centaxbooks.com

Introduction – Solutions

Several years ago, after moving into a newly built home, my Sansilvaria plant fell over, leaving a large brown stain on the carpet. I tried every commercial cleaner that I could get my hands on but the stain remained. Finally, I resigned myself to the fact that I would need to replace the carpet. Procrastination paid off because, three months later, a friend gave me a stain removal recipe to try. The ingredients in the recipe were items that I happened to have on hand. With nothing to lose, I carefully followed the instructions on the homemade recipe card and by the next day the stain was gone (see the recipe in Stain Removal Tips on page 46).

After that day I researched typical common household problems for each room in the house. I discovered hundreds of easy solutions for the kitchen, bathroom, laundry room, bedroom, garage and garden – all include the use of everyday household products. Not a day goes by that we do not face new challenges and decisions. Trying to juggle all of the elements in our lives is a task that can use simplification. The **Solutions** portion of this book provides answers to problems that occur daily. "Use metal to remove the smell of onions from your fingers; apply cream of tartar and hydrogen peroxide to combat rust," these are only a few of the ideas that you can try at home.

Each **Solutions** subject is broken down into a list of fifteen tips, making this book easy to read and reference. You will learn tricks of the trade and family secrets that will take the hassle out of day-to-day living by saving you time and money. Use what you have on hand and get ready to take on the challenges of everyday life!

Acknowledgements:

Special thanks to: Margo Embury, Dan Marce and staff at Centax, Wade Nerbas, Austin Nerbas, Kyah Nerbas, Kristi Nerbas, Jordan Nerbas, Margret Malaviya, Rekha Malaviya, Jean Pare, Iona Glabus, Jim Toth, Esther Bast, Sharon Nerbas, Garry Nerbas, Wendy Sidloski and Jason Kopytko.

Also, special thanks to Kelly Taylor and the Winnipeg Free Press who first printed selected "Solutions" lists.

Table of Contents

Solutions

Table of Contents

15 Solutions for Reducing Indoor Pollution

Cleaning your furnace and ducts is one of the most effective steps in reducing the amount of pollen, animal dander, insect droppings, fungus, bacteria and dust in your house. Every time your furnace goes on contaminants circulate throughout the living environment causing potential health problems, especially for children and seniors. The duct system of new and newly renovated houses should also be thoroughly cleaned. Construction materials and drywall dust tend to seep into the ventilation system. Also, periodically have your house tested for levels of carbon monoxide, radon (a colorless, odorless gas) and formaldehyde (used in carpet backing, upholstery glue, certain types of insulation and pressed-wood products).

1. Furnaces fuelled by natural gas, propane or heating oil should be inspected at the beginning of each heating season. The chimney and the pipes running from the furnace to the chimney should be examined for obstructions, holes, cracks or corrosion.
2. Begin the heating season with a fresh furnace filter and replace it once a month for every month that the furnace is in use. All maintenance instructions should be followed carefully.
3. Burn hardwood instead of softwood in your fireplace, and no plastics or treated wood. Burn only well-seasoned wood.
4. Toss a handful of salt into your fireplace occasionally. It helps prevent soot accumulation and makes colorful flames.
5. Minimize the mess when cleaning out a fireplace. Once you are ready to take out the ashes, sprinkle moist coffee grounds over them. The ashes will bind together better while you remove them.

6. Leave interior doors open whenever possible to ensure proper airflow. When you improve internal circulation, you keep airborne contaminants from building up in closed rooms and prevent the development of wet spots that harbor micro-organisms.

   Note: Indoor air is 10 to 20 times more polluted than outdoor air, and household dust is often more dangerous than outdoor dust. (Environmental Protection Agency)

7. Open windows regularly to increase airflow. Open doors and windows even on the coldest and hottest days of the year to allow fresh air to circulate through the house. Remember, it's more energy efficient to change all the air at once instead of a little at a time.

   Note: Using an appliance to clean the air can be less effective and more expensive than opening a window. Most air cleaners are designed to remove smoke and dust but not gases, tobacco, odors or viruses and bacteria.

8. Reduce humidity levels in the bathroom, basement and kitchen; these are the main areas of the house where biological contaminants can easily build up. Some ideas include: cleaning the basement floor drain with a disinfectant, ventilating the attic and crawl space and making sure that the clothes dryer is vented to the outside.

9. Consider installing an automatic timer or thermostat as a way of providing periodic ventilation in the kitchen or bathroom when the humidity reaches a preset level. The exhaust fan should be run while the kitchen stove or dishwasher or bathroom shower are being used, and for another 10 to 15 minutes afterwards.

10. A kitchen exhaust fan needs cleaning every 6 to 8 months. Turn the power off at the fuse box. Detach the grill and soak in mild dishwashing detergent; if you are not able to detach it, sponge it clean. Unplug and remove the fan and motor unit. Wipe off the grease with a cloth. (Do not immerse metal and electrical parts in water). Wipe out and clean the fan opening with a dry cloth, replace the clean fan and motor unit and plug it in. Dry and replace the grill. Follow manufacturer's instructions if you have access to them.

11. If your window air conditioner is giving off a moldy odor, the drain hole may be clogged. Unplug it, take off the front panel, and look for the hole underneath the evaporator area. Clear the hole with a long wire, e.g., a wire hanger.

12. Placing plants in several rooms in your house will do more than add ambience. Spider plants have a natural attraction to carbon monoxide; the elephant ear and heartleaf philodendron are known to absorb formaldehyde, benzene and carbon monoxide; aloe vera is easy to take care of and is also good at lowering formaldehyde levels; chrysanthemums help to remove benzene from the air.

13 Close the toilet seat before flushing, airborne bacteria can spread. **Tip**: Don't keep toothbrushes close to the toilet because germs travel past the toilet seat with every flush.

14. Use cleaning products with the least amount of toxins: avoid chlorine bleach by itself or as an ingredient of another product, stay away from oven cleaners, keep air fresheners to a minimum, avoid aerosol sprays and do not buy shoe polish that contains nitrobenzene, trichloroethylene or methylene chloride.

15. If you have carpets, clean them professionally every 6 to 18 months, depending on the level of traffic. To maximize the time between cleanings, keep dirt outside with mats at each entry. **Note**: The average house contains over 40 pounds (18 kg) of airborne dust, with as much as 30 million particles in one cubic foot (0.28 cubic meters).

15 Inexpensive Ideas to Reduce Heating Bills

1. Install clean furnace filters and clean all air intakes and outflow ducts. A clean filter maximizes energy efficiency and improves air quality.
2. Cover or remove window air conditioning units for the winter.
3. If you take hot baths at night, leave the water in the bathtub until morning (not recommended for families with small children). This also adds moisture to the air.
4. Regularly sweep woodstove and fireplace chimney flues.
5. Vacuum your electric heating baseboard elements and make sure no furniture or drapery is touching these elements.
6. Install an automatic thermostat in your home. Program the thermostat to reduce the heat at night or when you are not at home by 5 to 10 percent. You will save over 10 percent on your heating bill.
7. Turn down the heat in unused rooms and partially close heat vents.
8. Leave your oven door open slightly after baking to release warm air (not recommended for families with small children).
9. Invest in foam covers and mount them behind electrical outlet covers.
10. If you do not have door sweeps, be sure to keep the cold out by placing a towel at the bottom of outside doors.
11. Replace damaged rubber, wood, vinyl and metal weather stripping around windows and also around the outside edges of pet doors.
12. Look for places to add insulation: the attic, unfinished ceilings, crawl spaces, basements. Commercial insulation is rated by its “R” value. The higher the “R” the better the insulation will perform.
13. Remove old caulk, clean the joint and add new caulk around windows. If you own a hair dryer, window insulation kits are an affordable way of warming up a room in minutes.
14. Ceiling fans can be used to vent hot air up during the summer. By reversing rotation direction warm air is drawn down during winter.
15. Allow as much sunshine as possible through your windows. Open curtains and trim any trees that are shading your windows.

15 Ideas for Turning Cold Weather Inside Out

1. Extreme cold can cause the water pipes in your house to freeze. If this is a concern leave all taps slightly open so they drip continuously.
2. To conserve heat close off unneeded rooms and stuff towels in cracks under doors. Close draperies or cover windows with blankets at night.
3. To maximize the benefits of a wood stove follow these steps when building a fire: Lay down crumpled up newspaper, place kindling over the paper in a crisscross pattern. Toss in scraps of split wood, e.g., pine, spruce, maple, birch or ash. Open the damper and light a roll of newspaper; hold it up to the chimney to create an updraft for the fire. Light the paper underneath the kindling and add larger pieces of split wood, leaving spaces for air pockets to keep the fire ignited.
4. To paint a woodstove use enamel spray paint made for high temperatures. Brush the exterior with a wire brush and wipe it down before applying paint. Read all instructions listed on the can before application.
5. Before burning wood be sure that it is very dry. Use wood that has been chopped and left to sit for at least 12 months to guard against creosote buildup.
6. Mix soft and hardwoods together when preparing to light a fire. Softwoods, e.g., pine and spruce, are great for getting the fire started. Hardwoods, e.g., ash, maple and birch, are better for lasting fires.
   Note: Birch fires burn very hot, which helps clean the chimney, while ash burns less hot but for a longer period of time.
7. Keep a box of baking soda near the fireplace or wood stove to throw on a chimney fire should one start. The soda will lower the temperature in the chimney and can help to put out the fire.
   Tip: Clean brick on fireplaces using vinegar and a sponge.
8. To clean wood-burning fireplaces, line a cardboard box with newspaper. Use a spray bottle filled with water to wet down the ashes until they are damp (the debris will settle and leave less dust in the air). Collect the ashes with a shovel and dump them into the box. Wrap the ashes in the newspaper and discard.

9. If you use a kerosene heater, always follow manufacturer's instructions. Use the correct amount of fuel; refill outdoors; keep the heater at least 3 feet (1 m) away from flammable objects and ventilate properly. **Note**: Fire hazards greatly increase in the winter because alternate heating sources are often used without following proper safety precautions.

10. **Instructions on how to wash wool blankets**: 1) Tumble dry blanket by itself for 3 minutes to remove dust (no heat). 2) Fill washing machine with lukewarm water and add ½ cup (125 mL) detergent. Run washer for 3 minutes. 3) Turn machine off. Add blanket and let it soak for 10 minutes Use your hands or a broomstick handle to turn blanket. Set machine to spin. Never use the agitator on wool blankets. 4) Remove blanket and fill machine with warm water and 1 cup (250 mL) vinegar. Let blanket soak for 3 minutes. 5) Spin to drain. Tumble dry on the air-only setting for 20 minutes. **Note**: To soften blankets, add a capful of hair conditioner to vinegar rinse.

11. Keep satin comforters from falling off the bed by sewing a piece of cotton across bottom of the comforter, tuck cotton under mattress.

12. When heading outside on a cold day, layer your clothing: 1) Light synthetic shirt, 2) Vest, sweater or fleece top, 3) Wind-resistant coat, 4) Insulated coat. Wear non-cotton lightweight long johns under a windbreaker or wool pant. **Tip**: Mittens are warmer than gloves.

13. On cold days, drinking a tall glass of water can help your body stay warm because your body needs water to keep blood pumping. People tend to become dehydrated without knowing it.

14. Warm your spirits with a simple recipe for **Homemade Chocolate Pudding**: In a microwave, heat 2 cups (500 mL) milk with ¾ cup (175 mL) sugar for 2 minutes. Combine 2 egg yolks, 2 tbsp. (30 mL) cornstarch and 2 tbsp. (30 mL) cocoa. Add to milk. Whisk and heat in the microwave on high for 2 minutes; stir and add 1 tsp. (5 mL) vanilla. Heat for 2 more minutes, or until thick. Serve warm or cold as a pudding, or as a pie in a graham crust or pie shell. Top with whipped cream.

15. Stock your house with a disaster kit and include: flashlight, extra batteries, battery-operated radio, bottled water, non-perishable foods, essential medicines, blankets (sleeping bags), non-electric can opener, fire extinguisher, first-aid kit, emergency heating equipment.

15 Points for Choosing Roofing Materials

1. If your roof is leaking, check the flashing around the chimney vents. Cracked or loose flashing is most often the culprit behind a roof leak.
2. Leaks are rarely located directly above the water spots on the ceiling. While it's still raining, check under the roof deck for a drip trail starting at a higher point.
3. Glue down a curling asphalt shingle with roofing cement. Wait for a warm day when the shingles will be pliable. Slowly lift the curled shingle and dab the cement under the shingle. Apply a weight to the shingle for 30 minutes.
4. To clean roof cement from your skin, clothing and tools, wipe with a rag moistened with paint thinner. Don't use kerosene.
5. When an old roof loses its luster and begins to dry out, you can temporarily prolong its life with an acrylic-, asphalt-, or aluminum-formulation roof coating also known as roof paint. Acrylic coatings add reflectivity to asphalt, slate, metal, and tile roofing and can be tinted to match or change the color of your roof.
6. One way to deter fungus growth on your roof is to trim back trees to allow sunlight and airflow to the roof. To remove fungus from the roof, spray with a solution of 50% chlorine bleach and 50% water.
7. **Asphalt** is the most common roofing material. Generally asphalt shingles last for 15 to 30 years. They are made from fiberglass and asphalt granules.
8. **Torchdown** is best suited for wet climates on low-pitch roofs. It is a rubberized asphalt rolled material which is torched onto a non-combustible base.
9. **Cedar shakes** are an attractive natural product and have a natural resistance to decay but they are quite expensive.
10. **Slate** is heavy and durable, fireproof and can last 200 years. Each tile is different and when combined in a group it is distinctive.
11. **Standing seam metal** is often used for commercial roofing because of its durability and resistance to fire. It is becoming increasingly popular for home use.

12. **Solar roofing** can be economical in areas where there is a lot of sunshine. Consider solar roofing if you need to supply power to a house that is at least a mile off the power grid. In that case, solar roofing is usually cheaper than installing power lines.

13. The pitch of your roof is a ratio of height to depth at 12 feet. If your roof has a 7:12 pitch that means that the height is 7 feet with a depth of 12 feet. A low pitch has a pitch of less than 4:12

14. The principle design feature of a roof is the slope. A gable roof has two slopes, with a triangular gable at each end. In a hip roof the gable becomes a section of roof sloping up to the ridge of the main roof. A shed roof slopes in a single plane from one end to the other. A flat roof has a slight single slope, without eaves.

15. A skylight on the north side of a house gives clear light without the glare of direct sun produced by a skylight on the east, south or west sides of the house.

15 Easy Energy and Money-Saving Ideas

1. Test the efficiency of your fridge or freezer door seal. Close the door on a piece of paper. If the paper slides out easily, you should replace the seal. **Tip**: By unplugging a second fridge, you will save just under $100.00 per year.
2. Save energy and money: front-loading washers use 40 percent less laundry detergent and water and 50 percent less energy than top loaders.
3. When every flashlight in the house has batteries that no longer work, make a moveable light by plugging an electric night light into an extension chord.
4. To fix a gash in vinyl floors, find an extra piece of vinyl flooring (the matching vinyl works best). Rub it against a food grater until you have a pile of fine dust. Mix the dust with clear nail polish and use it to fill the slit. It will blend when dry.
5. Reuse and recycle an old briefcase to hold tools, you can lock it and store it in the trunk of your vehicle.
6. If you are tired of scraping the ice off your windshield, rub a cut onion all over your window to keep ice from forming.
7. Avoid the frustration of safety goggles fogging up while you are wearing them by rubbing a thin coating of dishwashing detergent on the inside of the lens.
8. Instead of bagging ashes that build up in chimneys, fireplaces and barbecues, sprinkle them over flowerbeds or gardens, or over icy paths instead of using salt.
9. If bubbles appear when you spread varnish, the can may have been shaken or stirred, creating air bubbles that can ruin a smooth finish.

10. Here is an easy way to make dripless candles: Prepare a solution of 2 tbsp. (30 mL) of salt per candle in just enough water to cover them. Soak for 3 hours; rinse and let dry. After 24 hours the salt water hardens the wax, allowing the candles to burn cleaner.

11. When glue thickens in the bottle add vinegar, it acts as a glue thinner or glue remover.

12. For people who live in an apartment or building where they do not want nail holes in the wall, or in houses where the walls are plaster and difficult to hammer nails through, hang posters with dabs of toothpaste. It's (hopefully) a staple item and easy to clean off .
    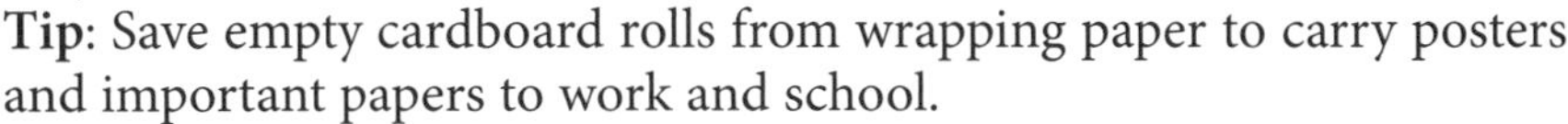
    Tip: Save empty cardboard rolls from wrapping paper to carry posters and important papers to work and school.

13. Painting the bottom of a door can be tricky when the door is on its hinges. Use a small piece of carpet to run paint along the bottom. Paint all 6 sides of the door to avoid expanding or splitting problems caused by moisture.

14. Here is an easy way to repair a shower curtain when the rings have pulled away. Cut a 2" (5 cm) by 1" (2.5 cm) piece of clear contact paper; fold it lengthwise over the tear. Use a hole punch to make new holes.

15. **Tape Magic:** To prevent plywood from splitting, attach a piece of masking tape to the spot where you will saw through plywood. The tape will keep the wood from splitting when you start cutting. **Tip**: Duct tape works well for lining leaky gutters and avoiding seepage.

Remember, there is always a solution when you own a role of duct tape.

15 Ways to Create a Toolbox You Can't Live Without

Start with a sturdy metal toolbox and add:

1. **Screwdriver – Multipurpose:** with retractable bits or a flat tip. Flat end screwdrivers fit tightly into many screw heads. If you use a screwdriver frequently invest in a cordless drill.
2. **Latex Gloves**: Wear them while painting or washing.
   Note: Be careful when wearing latex gloves, some chemicals will actually disintegrate them (I learnt that the hard way).
3. **Safety Glasses**: Protect your eyes against harmful chemicals and particles. It is also a good idea to wear **earplugs** when working around loud machinery.
4. **Crosscut Saw**: Cut wood to length using a saw with 6 to 8 points per 1" (2.5 cm). Wax the blade of a handsaw with a candle and it will cut through wood easier.
5. **Putty knife:** 3" (8 cm) for spreading and smoothing plaster. Clean plastic putty knives also come in handy when removing stuck-on food in the kitchen. A 1" (2.5 cm) metal scraper removes paint and nails.
6. **Fasteners**: Store a variety of fasteners and anchors so that you always have the proper size.
7. **Needle-Nose Adjustable Pliers**: Before making this purchase check to make sure that the pliers have wire cutters on the inside. Use needle-nose pliers to turn, grip, cut or pull objects.
8. **10-Foot Measuring Tape and String**: Use string to measure distances in unusually curved areas or when you are working alone. Tape the string to one end of the room or item that you need measured, guide the string to the other end and then measure the string.
9. **Adjustable Wrench**: For tightening or loosening nuts and bolts. The ideal wrench adjusts to 1¼".
10. **Hammer**: Light ones will do the trick for driving and removing nails.
11. **Flashlight**: Fill it with long-lasting batteries. **Tip:** Keep batteries in the fridge, they will last longer.

12. **Sandpaper**: Glue a piece of sandpaper around a block of wood to ensure an even surface on the wood you are sanding. **Flat file**: Metal file that smoothes out metal edges or surfaces.
13. **Variety of Tapes**: Electrical, duct, painters, masking and foil, for fixing gaps. **Glue**: use **white glue** for wood-to-wood interior projects; **contact cement** for laminate, veneer or material on wood projects; **epoxy** for metal on metal; **instant glue** for plastic, ceramic, glass and rubber.
14. **Small Torpedo Level**: Use for checking vertical and horizontal measurements. Often used when hanging pictures.
15. **Utility Knife**: Use for shaving wood and cutting carpet, linoleum, cardboard and plastic.

Remember, good-quality tools are a great investment. Take good care of them and they can last you a lifetime. Inexpensive tools cost you more in the long run because they do not last as long or work as well. A variety toolbox makes a great housewarming or wedding gift.

15 Earth-Shattering Glass and China Tips

1. After repairing a glass or ceramic object, lay it in a box of sand to hold the pieces together at the proper angle.

2. When washing delicate crystal, rinse in 1 part vinegar to 3 parts warm water. Air dry. To dry crystal immediately, use 3-day-old (or older) newspaper.
3. A combination of vinegar and lemon juice or baking powder and lemon juice will also clean crystal.
4. For really tough stains on crystal vases, etc., put 2 tsp. (10 mL) rice inside vase; add ½ cup (125 mL) water and swirl around gently. Repeat.
5. The following recipe is a powerful **window and mirror cleaner**: Combine equal parts rubbing alcohol and white apple cider vinegar in a spray bottle. Shake and spray. Wipe glass in a circular motion using paper towel.
6. Store mirrors and glass tabletops in a sturdy crate on edge as opposed to on a flat surface.
7. Pack glassware for moving by wrapping each piece in damp newspaper. Let the paper dry to form a protective cast around the glass.
8. Liven up china and glassware displays in a cabinet or shelf. Instead of piling plates and bowls together and organizing all wine glasses in a row, mix up pieces to create interest (after all it is a display). Use trays to showcase and frame special pieces. Stand a mirror behind glassware as an interesting background. Alternate china and glassware with books, napkins, photo frames, wine bottles, candles and baskets.
9. Tired of painting on paper? Why not try china painting? China painting, also known as porcelain painting or overglaze painting, is a technique which uses very thin washes to paint already-glazed pieces of glass. After painting, the pieces are fired in a kiln so that the color will not fade. This type of painting is often seen on antique china as well as tea cups. Ask your local ceramic store owner if they can help you with your first project. Check the Internet for detailed instructions.

10. When repairing glass and porcelain choose from these basic types of glue: **Silicone adhesive** – used on nonporous glass and porcelain. It will permanently seal stress cracks and breaks and also holds up in dishwasher heat and freezer cold. **Household cement** – not as strong as silicone, used on porous crockery and is highly flammable. **Epoxy putty** – dries in 30 minutes and can be used to build up a missing piece. **Epoxy gel** – dries in10 minutes and seeps into pores to create a very strong bond.
11. Remove black marks on china by using cooktop cleaning cream for smooth range tops.
12. To reduce stains on drinking glasses use a lime and scale remover product. Look for cleaners that are non-toxic and safe to use on dishes.
13. Clean utensil marks on china (caused by metal rubbing on glaze), with toothpaste.
14. Casseroles with stuck-on foods can be cleaned by filling the dish with boiling water and adding 1 tbsp. (15 mL) baking soda. Let sit for 2 hours and rinse.
15. Having a party and need to keep track of which drinking glass belongs to whom? Write the name of each guest on tumblers or mugs using nail polish. Rub with nail polish remover to erase the names after the party or fill them with candies and give them out as parting gifts. **Tip:** This idea is also a neat substitute for place cards.

15 Household Secrets . . . Revealed

1. When tomatoes get too soft to slice, chop them up and add a few minced cloves of garlic. Cook in the microwave on high for 3 minutes, stirring once or twice. Freeze and keep on hand for a quick tomato sauce.
2. To mix powdered drinks in a pitcher or jug, fill one-quarter of the container with water before adding the powder and sugar. Stir vigorously until dissolved. Stir in the remaining water. This way your drink is thoroughly mixed but you avoid the problem of splashing it all over your kitchen.
3. You can tell if your fridge is not cold enough by doing the butter test. Gently press your finger onto a refrigerated slab of butter, if it shows a dent the fridge is too warm, turn up the dial.
4. Double the number of uses you get out of steel wool soap pads; cut the pads in half after you buy them. Apply the same treatment to fabric softener sheets.
5. Prevent garbage bags from dropping into the garbage can, cut the elastic waistband from a pair of pantyhose. It makes an ideal giant elasticized band that you can stretch over the rim of a garbage can to hold the bag in place.
6. **Make your own handy wipes**. Use 1 roll of paper towels, 2 cups (500 mL) water, 2 tbsp. (30 mL) baby shampoo and 1 tbsp. (15 mL) baby oil. Cut the roll of paper towels in half and take out the cardboard center. Mix the water, shampoo and oil in an empty baby wipe container. Put half of the roll of towels in the container and press down to soak up the liquid.
7. Throw away your toothbrush when you're getting over a cold, strep throat or an upset stomach. The germs that made you sick can linger on your brush for weeks. An alternative is to run the toothbrush through the dishwasher.

8. To clean tough toilet bowl stains, try using unsweetened Kool-Aid in the bowl. It works wonders!
9. Take the guesswork out of linen closets. Before storing bed sheets, mark each different size by stitching colored yarn onto the hem, e.g., yellow for double, green for king, red for queen.
10. Protect your magazine collections by storing them in empty cereal box containers.

11. Dust a computer keyboard using a slightly dampened paintbrush to get into the little crevices. Or blow the dust away with a hairdryer.
12. Get rid of scratches on a compact disk by spreading the CD with peanut butter and then wiping with coffee filter paper.
13. A smart way to keep track of how much leftover paint is inside a paint can is to fasten an elastic band around the outside of the can at the paint level. Adjust the band as the level changes.
14. Do not buy a used furnace. It may be cracked and damaged and sized improperly (bigger is not necessarily better).
15. For icy steps in freezing weather, combine warm water with Dawn dishwashing liquid. Pour over the stairs – the solution won't refreeze. Carefully test before walking on the area.

15 Hints for the Frugal Shopper

1. Save money on food by planning suppers one month at a time. Be sure to factor in leftovers and days that you are likely to go out to eat. You will spend less time at the grocery store and save money because people usually pick up extra food with every shopping trip. Another advantage is that you won't need to make daily decisions about supper menus and you will probably eat out less.
2. Save on brown sugar by making your own. For every 1 cup (250 mL) of white sugar mix in 2 tbsp. (30 mL) molasses (costs about 40% less).
3. Instead of buying a pastry bag for cake decorating, use what you have. Roll a large piece of aluminum foil in the shape of a funnel, handle as you would a pastry bag (discard after each use). You can also fill a sandwich bag with frosting and cut the tip off one corner.
4. **Make your own flypaper**: Combine ¼ cup (60 mL) maple syrup, 1 tbsp. (15 mL) brown sugar and 1 tbsp. (15 mL) granulated sugar. Punch a hole on one end of a strip of brown paper (from a paper bag); tie a string through the hole. Let the paper soak in the mixture overnight. Hang.
5. Don't throw out candles that have lost their "new look." Instead, spray furniture polish onto a cloth and wipe the candle to give it new shine.
6. Save dried-up highlighters and bring them back to life. Remove the plug at the end of the highlighter. Add colored water to the inside and recap.
7. When the bristles on your shoe polish brush stick together. Soak the brush in paint thinner for six to eight hours and rinse well.
8. If you need clothespins in a hurry, use hairclips or clip-on earrings as a replacement.
9. To keep paint from spreading onto your child's sleeves during an art project (thereby having to buy new clothing or spend money on laundry detergent), cut the toe part off tube socks and slide the tube part onto his/her wrists.

10. Kids grow fast and seasons change, but before getting rid of clothes that are too small, cut the sleeves off winter jackets and wear them as spring vests.

11. No need to spend your hard-earned money on purchasing a piggy bank. Cut a slit on the bottom or back of an old teddy bear and use it to store cash (be sure that no one accidentally washes the teddy bear).
12. Cold creams soften leather just as well as expensive leather conditioning products. Rub on with your fingers and wipe off the excess.
13. When you cannot find the match to your favorite pair of earrings, wear one earring as a brooch instead.
14. For an inexpensive stain on raw wood, try tea. The stronger the tea the darker the stain. When dry, seal with a varnish.
15. When company is coming and you need an extra bed, pull the cushions off your couch and throw a bedsheet over all of the cushions. Tuck the corners of the bedsheet underneath the cushions just as you would if you were wrapping a gift. Secure the sheet to the cushions using safety pins.

15 Closet Storage Tips

1. Closet rods running parallel to a wall need to be about 12" (30 cm) from the wall for hangers to be at right angles to the wall. Rub a bit of furniture polish on clothes rods so hangers slide easily.
2. Don't hang sweaters, also avoid wire hangers.
3. Using a pant hanger, hang pants from the bottom or, to prevent creases, fold them over a hanger with a wide rounded bottom.
4. Suspend shower curtain hooks from closet rods to hold belts and bags.
5. To prevent table linens from creasing, install a rod just beneath a low shelf in a closet; hang linens on hangers padded with paper towel tubes.
6. Fold and store bed or bath linens by sets, not by size. It will be easier to find a complete set instead of searching through several piles.
7. Always place newly cleaned linens at the bottom of the stack to keep the same ones from being over used and wearing out.
8. When storing sheets, blankets or tablecloths, place the folded side toward the door.
9. Towels will look neat and take up less space in the linen closet if you roll them up like a jellyroll instead of folding them. Guest towels look especially pretty rolled in a decorative basket in the bathroom.
10. Your antique linens deserve to be treated with care; line shelves or drawers with acid-free tissue paper to keep fabric from yellowing. Linen storage spaces should be clean and painted; unfinished wood may stain fabrics over time.
11. To encourage neatness in children's closets, use plastic storage bins or boxes. Label them with pictures of what's supposed to go in them.

12. Store bins under the bottom shelf of a closet. To make quick and inexpensive storage bins, cover cardboard boxes with stick-on paper (you can match your shelf paper).
13. Create an office or sewing area inside a closet. Hang a peg board along the back wall of the closet and, using a length of wood slightly narrower than the depth of the closet, create a desk or table by mounting brackets for the wood to sit on.
14. To maximize space, get rid of linens you don't use. If you reserve old sheets for drop cloths or rags, keep those in the garage or basement.
15. Everything you own should have a home. Keep a bag in your closet for items you no longer use; when it is full drop it off at a charity bin.

15 Solutions for Blankets, Mattresses and Zzzzz's

1. **To ensure better sleep patterns:** Don't nap during the day; don't exercise just before going to bed; don't drink caffeine or alcohol for several hours before going to bed. Do maintain a regular schedule – go to bed and wake up at the same time every day.

2. **To get to sleep quicker**: Begin with a hot bath; listen to soothing music; drink a cup of warm milk or herbal tea; relax your mind. Forget about counting sheep (keeping track of 100 sheep jumping over a fence can stress out anyone) instead, try thinking of the name of a fruit or vegetable starting with each letter of the alphabet.

3. When buying a new bed it is always a good idea to buy the box spring and mattress at the same time. The box spring absorbs as much as half of the total weight of the sleep set and acts as a shock absorber for your body. Both components, the box spring and mattress, are designed to work together to give you maximum comfort.

4. When you shop for a mattress take your time and lie down on the bed. One-third of your life is spent sleeping so look for comfort and support; make sure that the mattress is big enough for your body type.

5. Use a battery-operated shaver to remove pilling on worn mattresses.
   Note: If you feel achy and sore each morning you may want to consider purchasing a new mattress.
   Tip: Turn your mattress frequently to equalize the support. Every two weeks for the first three months and every two months after that.

6. Alternatives to a standard headboard:
   - Purchase a beautiful curtain rod and hang fabric behind the bed.
   - Position a shoji screen with three panels at the head of the bed; leave it plain or decorate with photographs.
   - Cover a large piece of wood with batting and use a staple gun to cover the batting with fabric to match the bedding.

7. Measure your bed before you buy sheets. Standard bed dimensions: twin (single) 39" x 75" long; full (double) 54" x 75" long; queen 60" x 80" long; olympic queen 66" x 80" long; king 76" x 80" long or 72" x 84" long.

8. Check the thread count before purchasing sheets for yourself or as a gift. Anything over 250 TPI (thread count per inch) is comfortable, higher thread counts equal better quality (avoid under 200 TPI).
9. There are oversized sheet sizes to fit extra-cushiony mattresses. However, if you choose to use the sheets that you already own, you can add a wide elastic around the bottom of the sheet to make it fit. Or, slit the corners of a fitted sheet; cut open tube socks and sew sock sections into each seam.
10. To wear sheets evenly, place a safety pin on the bottom end of your sheet. After you wash your sheets move the safety pin to the other end of the sheet and again put the sheet with the safety pin on the bottom end of the bed.
11. If you agree that changing the sheets on bunk beds is time consuming, here is a tip for you. Select the sheets and blankets that you want to use for the bed and convert them into fitted sheets and blankets by adding elastic to the bottom hem. It may sound like a lot of work but think of the time that you will save in the long run.
12. Instead of throwing out an old sheet, keep the fabric and convert it into soft pajamas, dust rags, play clothes, curtains, emergency tensor bandages. Use it for bundling up an artificial Christmas tree, covering old furniture, as a tablecloth for messy art projects, bandannas, pillow cases or drop cloths for painting.
13. To remove the musty smell from stored blankets, sprinkle them with baking soda and roll them up for three hours. Shake the baking soda off and fluff up the blankets in the dryer on a no-heat setting.
14. Never dry a foam pillow in the dryer. Hand wash in lukewarm water, squeeze out excess water and dry the pillow in a cool place, away from direct sunlight, so that it does not turn yellow. A feather pillow may be washed with warm water and dried in a dryer on a low setting. Open the seam and add new feathers as desired. Sew up the opening.
    Tip: When resting on a pillow your head should be in line with your shoulders, in the same position as when you are upright.
15. Always check care labels before tossing teddy bears into the washing machine. Avoid the cost of dry cleaning your fuzzy friends by putting them into the freezer for a couple of hours to kill bacteria. Or use a garbage bag and shake them up with ¼ cup (60 mL) of baking soda.

15 Paper Cuts You'll Like

1. Tape a large envelope to the last page of your wall or desk calendar. Store papers that coincide with specific dates, e.g., field trips, golf tournaments, etc., inside the envelope. Using an "E," mark the calendar on special dates to remind yourself that details about the event are inside the envelope.
2. Instead of saving various-sized clippings from magazines and newspapers, photocopy them and put them into a binder. You will be more likely to refer to them if they are organized with tab headings.
   Tip: When labeling paper files avoid using the word miscellaneous. Be specific and concise with each subject.
3. Store valuable papers in tightly sealed plastic bags inside your chest or stand-up freezer. It is fireproof and a good hiding place. This is especially useful with freezers that lock.
4. Save business cards in a small photo album and sort them alphabetically or in business categories.
5. If you ever sift through papers not knowing whether to throw them out or store them, try both. Keep a large plastic box in a closet or in the basement or garage and fill it with papers that you think you will no longer need. At the end of the year go through the box and make a final decision on the papers.
6. When storing books they should stand vertically on shelves. Angling books adds stress to their structure and can cause them to become deformed. Large oversized books are best laid horizontally in stacks no more than 2 to 3 books high.
7. To pack books for storage, do not wrap in plastic wrap, garbage or cleaner bags because these emit harmful gases as they degrade. Use strong alkaline corrugated cardboard and allow 4" (18 cm) spaces between the boxes, walls, ceilings and floors. Place boxes on wooden pallets (do not store boxes on concrete floors).
8. If books get wet the affected material needs to be stabilized as rapidly as possible. Mold growth is likely to occur if the temperature is over 70°F (21°C). Freeze wet books and later dry them by standing them up, fanned open. Once dry, place books flat with a weight on top to minimize warping.

9. Cover dingy lampshades with new wallpaper and seal with varnish.

10. Line shelves with ungummed paper because sticky shelf liner attracts insects and is hard to remove. **Tip**: As an alternative use damp waxed paper, it adheres to the shelves, is easy to wipe off and is inexpensive.

11. Use paper to remove grease spots. Lay a piece of blotting paper over the spot and iron with a warm iron.

12. Keep your rolling pin wrapped in waxed paper and in the fridge. It will be chilled and ready to roll out pastry.

13. Consider installing paper towel racks in several places, e.g., bathrooms, workshops and basement. Paper towels transfer fewer germs and clean up messes in a hurry. **Tip**: Use a wet paper towel to mop up broken glass slivers.

14. Form any shape sculpture or piñata with this easy **papier mâché** recipe: Begin with 1 cup (250 mL) of water; mix in about ¼ cup (60 mL) flour until the mixture is smooth and thin. Stir in 5 cups (1.25 L) lightly boiling water. Boil for 2 minutes. Cool until warm. Dip strips of newspaper into flour mixture and drape over your mold. A balloon is the most common starting point, using many layers of paper and a little paint can give you a wide array of creations.

15. Paper napkin folding is simple and makes a great conversation piece at dinner parties. Use the following steps and a square napkin to create a **Bird of Paradise:**
    1. Fold the napkin in half and then in half again, forming a square with the four free corners at the bottom diagonally on a flat surface.
    2. Fold the bottom corner up to the top corner to create a triangle.
    3. Fold the right point down to the imaginary center line. Finger press the fold. Do the same on the on the left side.
    4. Fold the right bottom point underneath the napkin. Finger press then repeat on the left.
    5. Gently fold the napkin in half; the center will open slightly.
    6. Holding the broad end of the napkin closed by pushing it into the tines of a fork after the napkin folding is complete. Lift the four layers one at a time. The layers should be staggered and slightly curved. Voila!

15 Tips to Liven Up Bored Games

1. Start games by creating an unusual way to decide which player should begin first. Draw straws or have everyone attempt to say the alphabet out loud backwards, whoever says it the fastest and with the fewest number of mistakes begins.
2. Family Games Night or Friendly Games Night is an inexpensive way to have loads of fun. The rules are: Everyone chooses a game to play; it might be a board game, a relay race or questions and answers. Set the clock, the first facilitator explains the rules to his/her game. Play for 10 or 15 minutes (until the buzzer rings) and then everyone advances to the next person's game. The rules are that everyone has to be positive and (if possible) everyone must participate in each game.
3. Make a rule that everyone must shake hands and congratulate the winner after every game, and that the winner has to clean up the game. That way the losers can gracefully exit the room while the happy victor has a small job to do.
4. Board games can easily be forgotten when they are stacked on shelves in storage rooms. Encourage usage by choosing one game each week and leaving it in a highly visible area of the house such as the family room coffee table.
5. Most board games are coated with a glossy finish that can be cleaned by gently wiping with a damp sponge or cloth. Chinese Checkers boards may be vacuumed to avoid a buildup of dust inside each hole.
6. Organize game pieces in sealable freezer bags to keep them from getting lost. Also, using clear packing tape, secure game instructions to the inside lid.
7. If you want to hold a lid and game-board box together use yarn or ribbon as an alternative to elastic bands that tend to ruin the box.
8. Place clear wide tape along the seams of game boards before they tear, and also on each corner of game and puzzle boxes and lids.
9. If the spinner for your game breaks, drill a hole through a Popsicle stick and attach it to the cardboard with a nut and a short bolt. For a special treat, you could use jelly beans, smarties or gumballs as game counters or playing pieces.

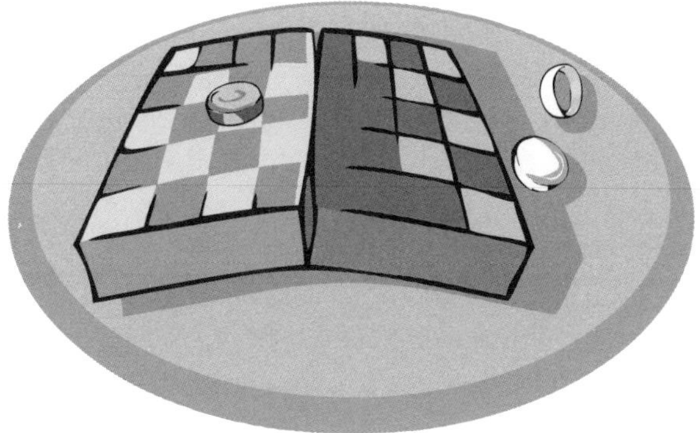

10. Rejuvenate dented ping-pong balls by dropping them into hot water for 2 minutes.
11. Make a cardholder by opening the flap of an aluminum foil box. Leave the cardboard roll in the box and align your cards in front of it. An alternative is to turn a shoebox (lid on) upside down. The cards can stand in the slot between the lid and the box.
12. To remove broken peg tips from a cribbage board, use a lit candle, heat a sewing needle and poke it through the center of the stuck peg. Pull it straight up.
13. Games stored at the cabin over winter may have a musty smell. Place fabric softener sheets in game boxes to keep them fresh.
14. To make it easier for players to see the dots on dice pieces, head to a Dollar Store and pick up a couple of large rubber dice.
15. A quick Internet search will show you many sites that describe and evaluate the wide assortment of new board games that are available.

15 Ways to Baby-Proof Your Home

1. **Playpens and Portable Cribs**: Use extra caution when purchasing used baby furniture. Make sure that there are no tears in the mesh or loose threads. The slats between rails should be no wider than 2⅜" (6 cm) apart. Do not leave the sides of a playpen down; make sure that each bracket is locked into place so that it will not collapse. **Tip**: Want to put an end to your child trying to climb out of the crib? Sew a piece of cloth on the outside crotch area of the sleeper in a triangle shape. He/she will not be able to lift his/her legs high enough to climb out.
2. **High Chairs**: Most high chair injuries occur when babies are not strapped into the chair properly (four to five deaths occur each year when babies slip under the tray and fall out). The chair should have a waist and crotch safety strap as well as a clamp that locks onto the table.
3. **Stairs**: More than half of all nonfatal injuries to children occur from falls. Install safety gates at the top and bottom of stairs. Be sure to use a gate that latches onto the wall because a toddler's weight is enough to push over a pressure-mounted gate.
   Note: Moveable walkers are illegal in Canada; in the U.S. walkers cause more injuries than any other type of nursery product.
4. **Toilets**: Hazardous because toddlers can drown in only a few inches of water. Use toilet lid locks or keep the bathroom door closed.
5. Cleaning buckets, bathtubs and diaper pails with even a little water should always be kept out of reach of toddlers.
6. **Plastic Bags**: Grocery bags should be kept away from babies and also dry cleaner bags, goody bags, the bags that diapers are sold in, garbage bags and whole or broken pieces of balloons. Also, umbrellas with hook handles can get caught in a child's mouth; although not fatal it is painful.
7. **Stoves, Dishwashers and Refrigerators**: Install locking latches on all appliances that open and close. Cover door handles with baby-proof covers. Turn pot handles in when cooking and try to use only the back burners whenever possible.

8. Cabinets and drawers contain a multitude of hazards, e.g., sharp objects, medications, cleaners, etc. Install latches to the insides of cabinets whenever possible. **Tip**: If you do not have childproof cabinet locks, attach one or more heavy rubber bands to the cabinet knobs in a figure-eight pattern.

9. **Electrical Cords**: If a toddler mouths a cord, even the smallest break can cause electrocution or burns. Buy cord bundlers to secure cords to furniture so they cannot be pulled.
Note: Studies have shown that some toddlers are able to remove ordinary plastic electrical outlet covers. Install tamper-resistant outlet face covers all over your house. Carry extras with you when you visit grandparents' and friends' houses that may not be baby-proofed.

10. Save bubble wrap for covering sharp corners on furniture. Use a strong tape to secure it so that the child is unable to pull it into his/her mouth.

11. **Fireplaces**: Install fireplace guards around a fireplace or, better yet, do not light fires while toddlers are in the room. Place a hearth cushion around sharp edges. Never leave a child unattended near a fire.

12. **Plants**: Be aware of the types and locations of your plants. Many are poisonous and can cause illness or death. Less obvious dangers are potting materials such as loose soil, moss, rocks and marbles.

13. **Water Heaters**: According to The Foundation for Burned Children, scalds are the leading cause of serious injuries in the home from birth to age four. Set the thermostat at 120°F (49°C) or less. Use your wrist to test water temperature before placing a child in the tub.

14. **Smoke Detectors**: Two-thirds of house fires occur in homes with no working smoke detectors. Install a combination of battery-operated and electrical smoke detectors on every floor as well as outside each bedroom. Replenish batteries with every time change.

15. **Windows**: Install window guards that only allow a window to open a few inches. Move all furniture away from the window. Purchase cord winders for blinds. Good-quality blinds typically come with a warning about the hazards of dangling cords. Other options for cords are: shorter cords, breakaway cords (if something gets caught in the cord it opens) and straight wands. One of the best innovations is the cordless horizontal blind that glides up and down with the pressure of your hand, excellent for kids' rooms!

15 Tips and Tricks for Kids

1. Before removing band-aids soak the area with baby oil. (Always keep baby oil out of reach of youngsters. Drinking baby oil can be fatal.)
2. To help children take medicine that they are not fond of, hold an ice cube on their tongues for a few seconds before offering medicine.
3. When children are not old enough to chew gum, you can still help soothe sore ears during an airplane ride by giving them a damp cloth or a soother to suck on.
4. Babies who are teething will enjoy chewing on a stripped corncob or the bristles of a toothbrush.

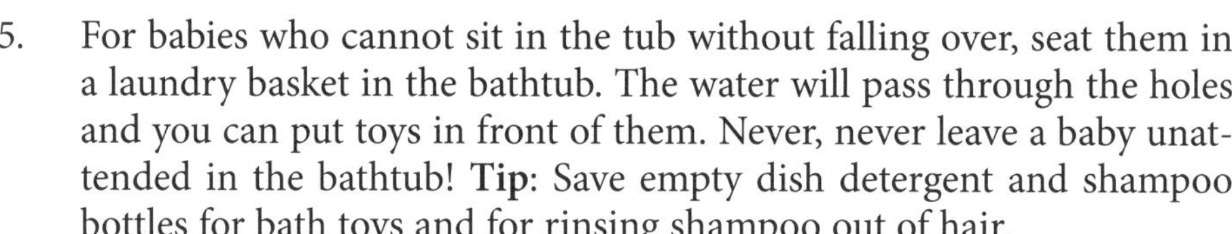

5. For babies who cannot sit in the tub without falling over, seat them in a laundry basket in the bathtub. The water will pass through the holes and you can put toys in front of them. Never, never leave a baby unattended in the bathtub! **Tip**: Save empty dish detergent and shampoo bottles for bath toys and for rinsing shampoo out of hair.
6. Put a rubber-backed bathmat over the edge of the bathtub to help prevent children from slipping when getting in and out of the bathtub. This also works well for seniors.
7. Encourage kids to help out in the kitchen. Use different-colored washcloths for various kitchen jobs. To reduce the spread of germs, choose one color for wiping counters and spills, another for cleaning dirty hands and faces, and yet another for scrubbing sinks.
8. To cool down soup or oatmeal in a hurry, put an ice cube in the bowl. Prior to learning to eat soup with a spoon you may want to give a child a straw to slurp up the liquid.

9. To assist your child to learn how to use chopsticks, fold a paper and position it between the chopsticks at the wide end (this keeps them from sliding), next, wrap a rubber band at the top to hold them together.
10. Keep the string from getting tangled up in the wheels of a pull toy by pushing the string through a straw and tying a knot on top to hold the straw in place.
11. Glue magazine pictures to the front of dresser drawers to help children understand where to find specific clothing items.
12. Remove gum from shoes and clothes by putting them in the freezer for an hour.
13. Reuse baby wipe containers by filling them with baby wipe refills. After your kids have outgrown the baby wipe stage (although keeping a container in the car can sometimes come in handy), fill the empty container with: crayons, photos, puzzle pieces, recipe cards, clothes pins, buttons, first-aid necessities, bookmarks, a secret stash of chocolate, old check books, etc.
14. Run out of bread for making sandwiches or just interested in shaking things up? Serve lunch in an ice cream cone. Select salmon, tuna, egg salad, peanut butter, cottage cheese or yogurt fillings, depending on your taste buds.
15. You can also make **individual birthday party cakes** by pouring cake batter into empty flat-bottomed ice cream cones. Leave ½" (1.3 cm) at the top. Stand cones in a muffin pan but be careful when putting them in and taking them out of the oven because they tip over easily. Bake at 350°F (180°C) for 20 to 25 minutes. Top with icing and Smarties, chocolate chips, peanuts or sprinkles. Candy Lifesavers on a cake create colorful tasty candleholders for children's birthdays.

    Cake Decorating Icing Recipe: In a mixing bowl, combine 3 cups (750 mL) icing sugar, 3 tbsp. (45 mL) milk, ¾ cup (175 mL) shortening (softened), 1 tsp. (5 mL) vanilla, and ¼ tsp. (1 mL) salt. Beat together, adding more icing sugar or milk as needed. Tint or leave white.

15 Squeaky Clean Tips

1. We all know that baking soda is a safe non-toxic household cleaning product. Following is a list of additional effective cleaners that serve important functions in your home:
   - **Lemon juice and white vinegar** – the acids dissolve gummy buildup, eat away tarnish and remove dirt from wood surfaces.
   - **Tea tree oil or lavender** – natural fungicides that remove mold as well as disinfect. Use 1½ tsp. (7 mL) to 2 cups (500 mL) water.
   - **Washing soda** – great for stubborn stains; cuts grease that builds up in the oven; cleans petroleum spills; removes wax or lipstick and reduces odor. **Caution:** Wear gloves when using. **Note:** Washing soda differs from baking soda in that it is stronger and caustic (that is why it is not used in cooking). Washing soda is sodium carbonate while baking soda is sodium bicarbonate. Washing soda will consume two equivalents of acid; baking soda will only consume one.
   - **Liquid Soaps and Detergents** – if you have hard water buy a biodegradable detergent without perfumes; if you have soft water you'll be better off using a liquid soap to cut grease.
2. **Clean and deodorize a microwave:** Fill a bowl with 1 tbsp. (15 mL) lemon juice and 1-2 cups (250-500 mL) water. Microwave on high for 5 minutes. Then, using a solution of 1 part baking soda to 4 parts water, wipe the inside and let dry.
3. **Shine wood floors:** Clean with a dust mop and then run the mop over the floors once again with a piece of waxed paper placed underneath.
4. Clean and wash doors before company arrives. Scrub with soap and water and wipe along the top edge, which is one of the most missed spots in the house (next to . . . the ceiling fan).
5. To polish bathroom fixtures, make a paste of 50/50 baking soda and dishwashing liquid. Apply and rub clean with a cloth (vinegar also works). **Tip:** To clean stains from bathroom chrome and tile, use baby oil. Wipe off with a soft cloth.

6. Do not dust hot light bulbs with a wet cloth because they could shatter. The same applies to television screens. Turn them off. Spray the cleaner on a cloth and then wipe the cooled glass.

7. Wash windows on cloudy but not rainy days. To remove spots on windowsills, rub the surface with rubbing alcohol.

8. The most efficient way to clean your home is to start at the top and work down, e.g., when you dust, begin at the highest point that you can reach and clean toward the floor.

9. Applying bleach products to toilet rings may not do the job. To remove an old ring, use a pumice stone dipped in water. Do not rub pumice stones on colored, enamel or plastic features.

10. Clean up bloodstains as soon as possible using a paste of water and cornstarch. Let dry and then brush off the residue.

11. Reduce hard-water stains on drinking glasses by rubbing them with steel wool dipped in vinegar.

12. To remove pet hair from upholstery, use a velour brush, vacuum cleaner or tape wrapped around your hand.

13. Spray a dust mop with furniture polish, the dust will be easier to collect when you sweep.

14. When cleaning ceramic floor tile, simply use soap and water. The trick, apply with a rubber squeegee instead of a cloth.

15. Plastic Polish by Novus is one of the best products on the market for removing the fine scratches, haziness and abrasions on: Plexiglas, plastic windows and windshields, cars, boats, planes, motorcycles, acrylic plaint, Fiberglass, tubs and showers as well as household plastics. **Caution**: Test in an inconspicuous area first.

15 Solutions for Tough-to-Clean Problems

1. To remove coffee stains from mugs, dissolve a denture tablet in hot water and allow it to cool. Soak overnight; rinse with vinegar and water.
2. To loosen hard-to-clean stains in glass or aluminum pots and pans, boil ¼ cup (60 mL) white vinegar with 1 cup (250 mL) of water in the pan for 5 minutes. Then wash the pan in hot soapy water.
3. To get rid of rust stains in the tub, mix ½ cup (125 mL) hydrogen peroxide with 1 tsp. (5 mL) cream of tartar; apply to stains. Wait 10 minutes and scrub.
4. Removing crayon marks from walls can be quick if you apply toothpaste to the mark. Wait 10 minutes and wipe.
5. If you never have time to relax with a bubble bath, use your bubble bath to wash walls. It cleans and lathers well, leaving a nice scent.
6. A plastic windshield ice scraper is handy for scraping dried-on foods off of the kitchen floor or table.
7. To whiten yellowed piano keys, wipe them with baking soda and water.
8. Recipe for an **All-Purpose Cleaner**: Put 2 quarts (2 L) of water in a bucket. Add ½ cup (125 mL) ammonia, ½ cup (125 mL) vinegar and ¼ cup (60 mL) baking soda.
9. Make your own **furniture polish**, mix ¼ cup (60 mL) vegetable oil with 2 tbsp. (30 mL) lemon juice. Rub on with a soft cloth.
10. To remove ink stains from white shirts, pour 7-Up over the stain. Wash in cold water.
11. For underarm perspiration stains on shirts, rub with deodorant soap before washing.
12. **Odor Removal**: Rub a lemon on your hands to get rid of fish smells; rub toothpaste on hands or clothes to remove the smell of diesel fuel.
13. Put pillows into a plastic bag, then into the freezer for 24 hours, to kill bacteria and dust mites.
14. To reduce dust, lay a fabric softener sheet inside the floor vents.
15. If you have an old trunk that smells musty, place an open box of kitty litter inside. Close the lid and let stand for a day.

15 Ways to Combat Rust

1. Remove rust on baking pans, tin, iron and other metals by scouring them with a raw potato and powered laundry detergent.
2. Rub kitchen utensils with a cork dipped in cooking oil.
3. Slice an onion through to the center. Move knives back and forth through the onion to remove rust.
4. Rust on clothes can be removed by holding a white pad under the stain, then applying lemon juice to the area and patting with salt.
5. Apply a mixture of vinegar and water to rust stains on carpets.
6. Rust stains in the kitchen and bathroom can be removed by soaking the area with coke. Leave overnight and wipe.
7. Coat tools with oil to prevent rust. If rust is present, remove it with a wire brush or sandpaper and then coat the tool with oil.
8. Tools won't rust if you store them in a mixture of sand and old motor oil.
9. Place several pieces of chalk or mothballs in a toolbox to eliminate moisture and prevent rust.
10. Soak a corroded bolt in vinegar for a few hours.
11. To prevent rust on chipped paint spots, clean the area and apply clear nail polish.
12. To paint wrought iron, apply one coat of aluminum paint and two coats of exterior paint.
13. If your car bumper has rust spots, dip aluminum foil into cola and wipe the rust spots.
14. Protect your trailer hitch from rust by cutting a tennis ball halfway though and placing it over the hitch.
15. In the spring, place a lawn sprinkler under your car. Let it run for 30 minutes to prevent salt from causing rust on your car.

Solutions

Over 60 Stain Removal Techniques From A-Z

A quick response to stains is often the key to positive results. Before attempting the following cleaning methods test a small inconspicuous spot of fabric, if positive results occur apply the method to a more noticeable area. The process of stain removable may not always be successful; the outcome often depends on how old the stain is.

1. **Alcoholic Beverages**: Blot immediately using a damp cloth, warm water and heavy-duty detergent. Let sit 10 minutes and wash as usual.

2. **Asphalt, Tar**: Cover area with ice and scrape away the tar. Apply dry-cleaning fluid (e.g., Shout) or turpentine to the back of the stain, placing fabric over absorbent paper towels. Rinse. Dab with heavy-duty laundry detergent. Wait 10 minutes and wash as usual.

3. **Automotive Oil**: Dab with ammonia or automotive degreaser; wash in heavy-duty detergent.

4. **Baby Food**: Dab meat tenderizer onto stain; let sit for 15 minutes. Wash as usual.

5. **Bacon**: Cover area with heavy-duty detergent or automotive degreaser; let sit for 15 minutes. Wash as usual; do not put into the dryer until the stain is gone. May need to be washed more than once before the stain disappears.

6. **Beets**: Treat stains as fast as possible and do not dry garment until the spot has disappeared. Soak a piece of white bread in cold water and lay over stained area, once the bread has absorbed the dye, wash fabric in color-safe bleach and heavy-duty laundry detergent.

7. **Blood**: **For washable fabric**, pour a small amount of shampoo onto stained fabric or apply a paste of powdered detergent and water; flush with cool water and scrub. Soak the stain until gone – this may take several hours – then wash as usual. For a persistent stain, wet area with water. **For dry-clean-only fabric**, dampen area with cool water; blot with a towel and take to a dry cleaner as soon as possible. Wet area with

¼ cup (60 mL) hydrogen peroxide and 1 tbsp. (15 mL) ammonia. Leave for 5 minutes, rinse with cold water. **Note**: Test an inconspicuous area of the fabric first.

8. **Butter**: Cover area with heavy-duty detergent or automotive degreaser, let sit for 15 minutes. Wash as usual, do not put into the dryer until the stain is gone. May need to be washed more than once before the stain disappears.
9. **Candle Wax**: Put item in the freezer. Scrape off as much of the wax as possible. Place stain between clean white fabric and press with warm iron. Apply a spot stain remover and wash as usual.
10. **Candy**: Mix 1 tsp. (2 mL) mild-detergent with 1 cup (250 mL) water. Blot. Mix ⅓ cup (75 mL) white vinegar with ⅔ cup (150 mL) water. Blot and wash as usual.
11. **Cheese**: Never put this protein stain in hot water. Presoak in cold; dab on ammonia and wash as usual.
12. **Chewing Gum**: Apply ice to harden the stain. Blot with lemon juice and scrape off the excess with a butter knife. Apply heavy-duty liquid detergent. Rinse and wash as usual. **Note:** Peanut butter also works, but then you need to deal with a grease stain.
13. **Chocolate**: Dab on heavy-duty detergent; rinse in cold water. Mix 1 tbsp. (15 mL) ammonia with ½ cup (125 mL) water. Blot and wash. If stain remains sponge with hydrogen peroxide and rewash.
14. **Chocolate Milk**: Never put this combination protein stain in hot water. Presoak in cold water and heavy-duty detergent; dab on ammonia and wash as usual.
15. **Coffee**: Use a Commercial stain remover, OR mix 1 tsp. (5 mL) vinegar in 1 quart (1 L) cold water. Sponge on stain, then launder. OR, work in beaten egg yolk and let sit for 10 minutes. Rinse with cold water. Next, stir 1 tsp. (5 mL) detergent into 1 cup (250 mL) water. Apply to stain. Rinse and combine ¼ cup (60 mL) white vinegar with ¼ cup (60 mL) cold water. Wash as usual.
16. **Correction Fluid**: Test small area on fabric before treating stain. Apply paint thinner or rubbing alcohol to stain. Wash as usual.

17. **Crayon**: Place stained side down on a pad of paper towels: spray with WD-40. Let stand 5 minutes. Turn fabric over and spray the other side. Work liquid detergent onto stain. Wash in hot water with laundry detergent and color-safe bleach.
18. **Deodorant**: Sponge stain with rubbing alcohol. Leave 15 minutes and wash as usual.
19. **Dirt**: Allow area to dry, brush dirt away. Slice a raw potato in half; rub onto stain; soak in cool water for 10 minutes. Wash as usual using heavy-duty detergent.
20. **Easter Egg Dye Stain Remover**: Mix ½ tsp. (2 mL) of dishwashing liquid with ½ cup (125 mL) of lukewarm water. Dab with a white cloth. Repeat. If the stain remains pre-test the following solution on a discreet area of the fabric. Mix 1 tbsp. (15 mL) ammonia with 1 cup (250 mL) water. Dab onto fabric. Rinse. Let dry.
21. **Egg (raw)**: Soak stain in cold water for 10 minutes. Wash as usual using heavy-duty detergent.
22. **Fabric Softener**: Remove by rubbing with a bar of laundry soap. Detergents do not seem to be effective in removing fabric softener.
23. **Feces**: Soak area in cold water. Launder in warm water using heavy-duty detergent and colour-safe bleach.
24. **Fingers**: Soak stained fingers in lemon juice or vinegar. Then brush skin with a toothbrush using soap and water.
25. **Fruit and Juices**: Mix equal parts white vinegar, dishwashing liquid and water in a squirt bottle and spray onto stain. Let stand for 10 minutes and rinse.
26. **Gelatin**: Soak area with cold water. Launder in warm water using heavy-duty detergent and color-safe bleach if the stain is colored.
27. **Grass**: Rub in toothpaste; let sit 15 minutes and wash as usual.
28. **Gravy**: Cover spot with cornstarch. Leave for 1 hour. Wash as usual.
29. **Grease/Oil**: Cover area with heavy-duty detergent or automotive degreaser, let sit for 15 minutes. Wash as usual. Do not put into the dryer until the stain is gone. May need to be washed more than once until the stain disappears.

30. **Hand Cream**: Act fast. Rub baking soda on area; let sit and dry. Brush away powder and wash as usual.

31. **Ink Pen/Marker**: Although hairspray is an effective way to get rid of ink, the hairspray mark may be difficult to remove. Blot the ink with glycerine or rubbing alcohol and wash as usual.

32. **Ink Stains in Dryer**: Depending on the type of ink and how long the stain has set, ink may be impossible to remove from the dryer drum. However, attempt to remove by wetting a rag with rubbing alcohol and wiping the inside of the drum.

33. **Ketchup**: Mix 1 tsp. (2 mL) mild detergent with 1 cup (260 mL) lukewarm water. Blot. Combine 1 tbsp. (15 mL) ammonia with ½ cup (125 mL) water. Blot and wash as usual.

34. **Kool-Aid**: Equal parts white vinegar, dish-washing liquid and water. Mix in a squirt bottle and spray onto stain. Let stand for 10 minutes and rinse. Or use carbonated water in place of vinegar.

35. **Lipstick**: Dab rubbing alcohol onto area; rinse with warm water. Pour a few drops of liquid dishwashing soap or stain remover on area. Wash as usual.

36. **Mayonnaise**: Make a runny paste of heavy-duty laundry detergent and water; work solution into stain. Let sit for 10 minutes: wash in hot water. Inspect before drying.

37. **Mildew**: Pretreat with heavy-duty detergent; launder in hot water. If the stain remains sponge on a combination of 50/50 lemon juice and salt; dry in the sun and wash as usual.

38. **Milk Products**: Never put this protein stain in hot water. Presoak in cold water; dab on ammonia and wash as usual.

39. **Mustard**: Apply glycerine or ammonia; let sit 10 minutes. Wash as usual.

40. **Nail Polish**: Acetate or triacetate fabrics must be dry cleaned. Otherwise, place fabric face down on paper towels, apply nail polish remover to the back of the stain and blot until it is gone.

41. **Paint (oil base)**: Treat while wet by removing with paint thinner, turpentine or rubbing alcohol. Wash with heavy-duty laundry detergent.

42. **Paint (water base)**: Needs to be treated no longer than 6 hours after spill. Apply commercial stain remover to fabric. Wash in cold water with heavy-duty detergent.

43. **Perfume**: Soak in equal parts hydrogen peroxide and water. Wash as usual.

44. **Red Wine**: Pour white wine or salt over stain or a mixture of 50/50 dishwashing liquid and vinegar. Let sit and wash as usual.

45. **Rubber Cement**: Remove using paint thinner, lacquer thinner or vinegar. Wash as usual.

46. **Rug Stains**: Apply a combination of 50/50 lemon juice and cream of tartar. See also **Fantastic Stain Removal Recipe**, page 46.

47. **Rust**: Check for colorfastness, sprinkle salt onto stain and spread lemon juice over top. Lay garment in the sun for a day.

48. **Salad Dressing**: Make a runny paste of heavy-duty laundry detergent and water; work solution into stain. Let sit for 10 minutes, wash in hot water; inspect before drying.

49. **Scorched Fabric**: Scorch marks are different from a true stain in that the fibers are permanently damaged. Very light scorch marks may be removed by immediately washing the area with heavy-duty laundry detergent followed by an application of hydrogen peroxide. Cover the stain with clear plastic wrap and weigh down with heavy books. Remove after 12 hours. Chances of removal are slim but it is worth trying. OR, try rubbing a raw onion on scorched fabric and let soak for a couple of hours. OR, remove scorches on fabric by wetting fabric and applying color-safe bleach before washing.

50. **Scuff Marks** (on vinyl): First try erasing the marks. Next, combine 3 tbsp. (45 mL) trisodium phosphate (found in hardware stores as TSP) to 1 gallon (4 L) water. Apply with an abrasive cloth.

51. **Silly Putty**: Spray WD-40 onto area, let stand for 5 minutes. Blot with rubbing alcohol and rinse. Before washing, spray with spot cleaner.

52. **Shoe Polish**: Wash with heavy-duty laundry detergent. If unsuccessful, apply glycerine and leave for 1 hour. Wash in warm water.
53. **Soft Drinks**: Soak spot in full-strength vinegar for 2 hours. Wash as usual.
54. **Soy Sauce**: Step 1: Blot with non-bleaching heavy-duty liquid detergent. Rinse. Step 2: Sponge with 1 tbsp. (15 mL) ammonia in ½ cup (125 mL) warm water. Rinse and repeat step 1.
55. **Suntan Oil/Lotion**: Apply heavy-duty laundry detergent and water; let soak for 10 minutes. Wash with hot water and heavy-duty laundry detergent.
56. **Tea**: Flush with lemon juice to remove the color. Next, wash, using a color-safe bleach combined with heavy-duty detergent.
57. **Tobacco**: Apply equal parts baking soda and water.
58. **Tomato Juice/Spaghetti Sauce/Salsa**: Sponge with cold water and a few drops of glycerine. Apply spot stain remover using a toothbrush. Wash as usual.
59. **Urine**: Sponge with 1 tbsp. (15 mL) ammonia in ½ cup (125 mL) warm water.
60. **Vaseline**: Make a runny paste of heavy-duty laundry detergent and water; work solution into stain. Let sit for 10 minutes; wash in hot water; inspect before drying.
61. **Vomit**: Sponge area with 1 tbsp. (15 mL) ammonia and 1 cup (250 mL) warm water. Wash as usual.
62. **White Wine**: Flush with cold water; wash as usual.
63. **Zucchini**: Mix equal parts white vinegar, dishwashing liquid and water in a squirt bottle and spray on stain. Let stand for 10 minutes and rinse.
64. **Unidentifiable Stain**: Dab stain with a solution of 3 denture tablets dissolved in 1 cup (250 mL) cold water. Wash as usual.
65. **All-purpose Stain Remover**: Combine 1 quart (1 L) borax with 2 cups (500 mL) cold water, soak fabric for 10 minutes; wash in cold water. **Note:** Never combine chlorine bleach with ammonia or rust removers. The mixture can create fatal toxic gases.

66. The majority of rug stains can be removed by simply drying the area with a light solid-colored cloth. Blot until the area is damp, then pile plastic wrap and heavy books on top. Wait for twelve hours; remove.

Fantastic Stain Removal Recipe for Carpets: I have used the following very effective recipe many times for pet, food and plant stains. In my experience no damage has ever occurred and the results have surpassed any of the commercial cleaning agents. However, use at your own risk, you should test a small area of carpet before applying the recipe. Some stains that have set for a long period of time are impossible to remove but it's worth a shot. Best Wishes!

1) Mix together ½ tsp. (2 mL) clear dish detergent and 1 cup (250 mL) warm water. Blot (do not scrub) onto stain and leave for 5 minutes. Pat area dry using a white paper towel.

2) Mix together ½ cup (125 mL) hydrogen peroxide and 2 tbsp. (30 mL) ammonia. Dip white paper towel in solution and blot onto stain. Cover the stain with clear plastic wrap and weigh down with heavy books. Make sure that the books are not touching the carpet because if the book gets wet the dye from the paper could seep onto the carpet. Leave 12 hours.

3) Blot dry

4) Blot with warm water and dry 2 to 3 times.

5) Dry with paper towel as much as possible. Air dry.

6) When dry, blot with white vinegar and leave.

15 Oily Solutions

1. If you use cooking oil often for cooking or cleaning, clean an empty liquid-soap pump bottle and fill it with oil.
2. Keep cats away from houseplants by soaking a cotton ball in cooking oil and hiding it in the soil.
3. To keep water away from a dog's eyes during a bath, rub a thin layer of petroleum jelly around his/her eyes before bath time.
4. Rub oil on your pet's fur to remove burrs.
5. Rub hair with peanut butter or oil to remove chewing gum.
6. Heat olive oil until warm and run the oil through your hair as an inexpensive oil treatment.
7. If your baby has cradle cap, rub a thin layer of cooking oil on his/her head. Let sit for two hours and comb the hair before shampooing it.
8. Conquer dry hands by covering them with a thin layer of petroleum jelly and wearing cotton gloves or socks on hands overnight.
9. Remove oil paint from hands by working cooking oil into hands. If you apply oil to hands before painting, the paint should not stick to you. Before painting, apply a small amount of oil to surrounding wood to keep any accidental paint smears from sticking.
10. Help zippers slide easily by applying a small amount of oil along the teeth (wax also works well).
11. Oil is a fantastic way to remove sticky decals. Rub the oil all around the sticker and let it sit for the afternoon before peeling off the decal.
12. Spread candleholder rims with petroleum jelly to keep wax from sticking. Rub petroleum jelly around the rims of paint cans and tubes of glue to keep the lids from sticking.
13. Rub petroleum jelly around the rim of toilet plungers, this acts as a seal when unclogging a toilet.
14. Apply petroleum jelly to the end of a stick to retrieve unreachable objects.
15. To prevent rust, spread oil liberally on tools, skates and fishing rods that are not used frequently.

15 Ways to Keep Fabrics Looking New

1. Although professional cleaners cannot eliminate all stains, the cleaner should warn you if a stain cannot be removed. However, this is difficult to predict. An already-washed dye stain is an example of a stain that is usually permanent.
2. Oil stains can typically be removed if quickly treated but, if oil stains become dried in the dryer or ironed, removal may be impossible. **Tip:** Liquid detergents are better at removing oil stains than powder.
3. Soften laundry by adding a cup of vinegar to the rinse cycle. Get white socks white again by boiling them in water with a slice of lemon.
4. Bleaches have a limited shelf life and may need to be replaced after 6 months. To test for colorfastness of liquid bleach, mix 1 tbsp. (15 mL) bleach with ¼ cup (60 mL) water. Drop onto hidden area and wait 3 minutes. If there is not color change it is safe to use on fabric. However, chlorine bleach diluted with water should be used as a last resort because it almost always alters the dye of a fabric as well as the stain. **Caution**: silk, wool and other hair fibers will dissolve in liquid chlorine bleach.
5. Bleaches come in a variety of forms. Some non-commercial choices are: lemon juice, white vinegar, 1 part hydrogen peroxide combined with 1 part water, or 2 parts water mixed with 1 part ammonia.
6. When one color bleeds into another color on the same garment, rewash the item in heavy-duty detergent with warm water before drying.
7. Avoid rubbing a fresh stain with bar soap. Soap can set the stain.
8. Do not use hot water on unknown stains. Hot water sets protein stains such as milk, egg and blood. Also, ironing stained fabrics can set stains. **Tip:** Often spot remover tips call for an enzyme presoak. An enzyme presoak is a pre-treatment product used to break down proteins like grass, blood and baby formula (most detergents contain enzymes). Product labels will advise consumers if a solution is specifically an enzyme presoak.
9. Before bringing a garment to a dry cleaner, write down any stain problem on a piece of paper and pin it to the spot. Otherwise, the garment may be cleaned without applying special treatment to the area.

10. Wash heavily soiled items separately because soil can be redeposited during laundry: if the amount of detergent is less than required; if water temperature is too low; if the washer is overloaded.
11. Remove stains and launder clothing using the required type of detergent. Examples of **heavy-duty liquid detergents** are: Tide, Whisk, Oxydol and Amway. **Light-detergents**: Ivory, Woolite and **powdered detergents:** Cheer, Tide and ABC.
12. If you do not know the origin of a stain, start by soaking the fabric in cold water. Next, wash with liquid detergent and warm water: air dry. If the stain persists, apply pre-treatment spray. If still not gone, dilute liquid chlorine bleach and water 50/50. Wash as usual.
13. Take 10 minutes off your drying time by shaking each item that comes out of the washer before loading it into the dryer.
14. To remind yourself to pre-treat a piece of clothing, tie a knot in the sleeve or pant leg before tossing it into the hamper.
15. Keep in mind that if you follow the label's directions and your clothing changes color or fades, the manufacture is at fault and should replace it. However, manufacturers sometimes include a statement on the label that acknowledges that changes in color are part of the product's charm. This covers them and warns you that color changes are likely to occur after the first or second wash.

15 Solutions That Leave Fabrics Feeling Sew Good

1. Buttons will stay on fabric longer if you dot the button threads on new garments with clear nail polish. **Tip**: Sew children's buttons on with dental floss.
2. When applying patches to the knees of pants that are used for gardening, add comfort by leaving the top of the patches open so that you can slip shoulder pads inside.
3. Before sewing a hem, cut a piece of cardboard the same width as you want the hem to be. Move the cardboard underneath the fabric while securing it.
4. Beginner tailors will benefit from this tip, instead of using straight pins to secure a hem, slide paperclips along the edge. Paperclips won't poke you and they are easy to remove. **Tip**: Ripping stitches from dark hems can be tricky because the stitches are difficult to see. Use a piece of chalk and draw over the hem before pulling stitches. The chalk will wash out easily.
5. Simplify your life by applying hairspray to the ends of thread before attempting to thread a needle.
6. If you spend time searching for sewing tools during projects, glue Velcro pieces to each tool, e.g., pincushion, scissors, bobbins, etc. Apply a long strip of Velcro to the wall or to the side of the sewing table and attach accessories to the strip. **Tip**: A handy idea for injecting oil into your sewing machine is to store the oil in a syringe.

7. Don't throw out your favorite garment just because it has a snag in the fabric. Consider making the same length snag on the opposite side of the garment as a design element. Apply fusible interfacing to the wrong side of the fabric. You can also stitch around the snags to emphasize them instead of trying to hide them.
8. Sharpen sewing scissors by cutting through a piece of aluminum foil several times. **Tip**: While on the subject of aluminum foil, place a piece of foil underneath your ironing board cover to reflect heat onto garments.
9. Instead of spending oodles of money on detergent for fine washables, make your own. Soak items in a sink of cold water for colors; warm water for whites. Add 1 tbsp. (15 mL) of hair conditioner. Leave for 3 minutes, rinse and hang to dry.
10. An easy way to prevent sweaters from stretching on a clothesline is to string an old pair of pantyhose through the arms and then pin the pantyhose to the line.
11. Bleached-out spots on clothing may be covered up using the same color fabric paint. The paint will not wash off and you can delay having to throw out yet another piece of clothing.
12. Keep clothes from falling off wire hangers by winding a rubber band around the corners of the hanger.
13. To store or travel with silk scarves, roll them around empty paper towel tubes. This will help avoid creases caused by folding.
14. To extend the life of pantyhose, wet them when new, and place them in a plastic bag in the freezer for a few hours.
15. To clean artificial flowers, pour salt into a paper bag and add the flowers. Shake well, the salt will absorb the dust.

15 Ways to Keep Leather Buff

1. Do not store leather in plastic, it can dry out. Cover leather with a pillowcase, sheet or other fabric.
2. Instead of applying expensive conditioners to soften leather, rub cold cream onto the leather and wipe away the excess cream with a towel.
3. When you find a stain or mark on a leather garment, use the inside cuff of the leather piece to rub against the stain.
4. If you get caught wearing leather in the rain, hang it to dry away from direct sunlight. Later, brush the nap back with a foam rubber block or pad. When leather clothing does need cleaning, take it to a professional. Never put leather in the dryer!
5. Hang leather garments on a padded, wooden or plastic hanger, do not use wire.
6. If you notice oily stains on your leather gloves, dust them with cornstarch and leave them overnight. Brush off the excess.
7. When storing tall leather boots, tie empty paper towel rolls together and slide them inside the boots to help them keep their shape and look new longer.
8. Take care when ironing leather, it may shrink. To iron leather, place the leather face down over a brown paper bag. Using a press cloth, iron on a low setting.
9. To prevent damage to leather, avoid putting it in direct sunlight, heat and in damp areas.
10. Avoid cleaning leather too often, only when necessary.
11. **To clean leather furniture**, mix ¼ cup (60 mL) vinegar and ½ cup (125 mL) water; use a cloth to wipe off wax buildup. To restore the shine use a circular motion and apply saddle soap to the leather.
12. Butter, oil or grease on leather furniture should be wiped off gently, using a dry cloth. Allow any remaining grease to absorb into the leather.

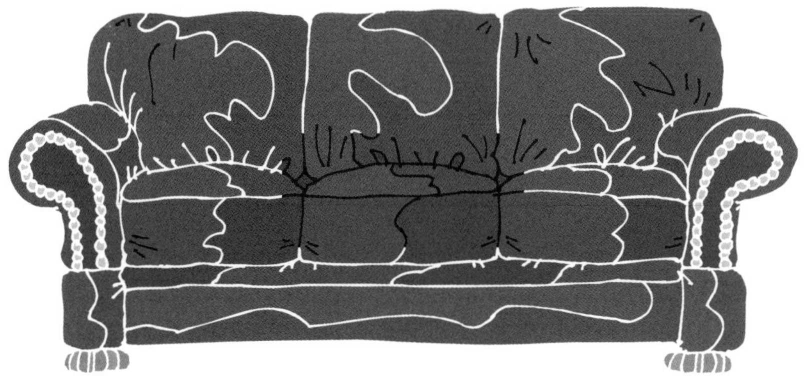

13. For bleach stains on a leather tabletop, clean the surface of the whole table with saddle soap and let it dry. Next, find a color of liquid polish that matches the tabletop as closely as possible and rub some onto the stain. If the color is too dark, lightly cover the entire surface of the table with the polish.

14. When purchasing leather furniture consider its usage. Do you have children or pets? If so, a lower-grade leather piece may be a wise choice for you. Lower-grade leather has a higher durability and more sheen because of the chemicals it is treated with (it feels rougher to the touch).

15. There are several grades of leather – the higher the grade the softer and more supple to the touch. You also need to decide whether you want the piece to be completely covered in leather or partially vinyl on the back. How do you decide? Cost is one factor, the higher the quality of the leather the more expensive it will be. Positioning is the other component; decide where the furniture will be placed in the room. If a loveseat is going to be against a wall, then the back shouldn't matter as much as if you place the loveseat on an angle with the back in full view. **Tip: Real versus Synthetic Leather** – If your budget allows, purchase furniture with top-grade leather, at least on areas where you will be making contact with it.

15 Soft Solutions

1. Rub a new fabric-softener sheet over slips, dresses, hairbrushes and pantyhose to prevent static.
2. Wipe your hair with a fabric-softener sheet to control static electricity. **Tip**: Keep an extra sheet in your purse during dry months.
3. **Make your own static eliminator:** Mix 1 part liquid fabric softener and 20 parts water. Store in a spray bottle.
4. Spray carpets with 1 part liquid fabric softener to 5 parts water to help prevent static shocks.
5. Eliminate static electricity from television and computer screens and Venetian blinds by wiping with a fabric-softener sheet to discourage dust from settling. **Note**: Clean up sawdust, cat and dog hair by rubbing the area with a fabric-softener sheet.
6. Used fabric-softener sheets can substitute for perfumed sachets.
7. Mask the smell of cigarettes in your house by filling and setting out bowls of vinegar or a mixture of 2 tbsp. (30 mL) ammonia in 1 cup (250 mL) of water. Also, lay fabric-softener sheets inside air vent grills.
8. Place fabric-softener sheets under car front seats to freshen air.
9. To eliminate musty odors, tuck fabric-softener sheets in old books, suitcases, sleeping bags, tents, vacuum cleaners and hampers.
10. Tie a fabric-softener sheet to your belt loop to repel mosquitoes. Also, keep bees away by putting a fabric-softener sheet in your pocket.
11. Lay fabric-softener sheets where ants and mice crawl to deter them.
12. Store used fabric-softener sheets in a jar with some liquid fabric softener. When drying a load of clothes, squeeze out the excess liquid from one of the sheets and add it to the dryer.
13. Drop a capful of liquid fabric softener into 1 quart (1 L) of water to make your own lint-free cleaner for regular glass and Plexiglas
14. Clean eyeglasses by wiping them with a fabric-softener sheet; this will also discourage them from fogging up. **Tip**: Wipe shower doors with a fabric-softener sheet to dissolve soap scum.
15. Buff shoes to a high gloss using a fabric-softener sheet.

15 Ideas for Steamy Shower Problems

1. Get rid of spiders in your bathtub by spraying bug killer into the overflow hole.
2. Apply acrylic floor wax to shower doors to make them shine.
3. Say goodbye to water spots on shower doors by drying them with dryer sheets.
4. To clean mildew off shower tiles, spray bleach onto paper towels and spread them on the walls. Leave towels on overnight and rinse the wall in the morning.
5. To repel soap scum and hard water deposits on fixtures, rub with baby oil.
6. When repairing or applying caulk around shower walls. Clip the end of the cartridge at an angle. Apply and smooth caulk with a wet finger.
7. To remedy a clogged showerhead, unscrew the head, take the pieces apart, and soak them in a bucket of vinegar. Scrub with a toothbrush and resemble.
8. Cut your water use in half by installing an inexpensive water restrictor or a water-saving showerhead.
9. Before hanging, soak shower curtain in a solution of salt water to avoid mildew.
10. To clean your shower curtain, soak it in baking soda and water.
11. Your shower curtain will slide better if you rub the rod with a bar of soap.
12. A quick fix to avoid slipping in the shower is to lay a towel on the bathtub or shower floor.
13. Organize your tub by hanging shampoo, bath toys and bubble bath in an ice cream bucket over your tub spout.
14. Place a sponge on top of the soap dish to avoid the dish getting caked with hard soap.
15. If you run out of shampoo, use glycerine soap as a substitute.

15 Solutions with Water

1. If your dishes are not clean when they come out of the dishwasher, the water may need to be hotter. Test the water by filling a bowl with hot water from a tap. Place a candy thermometer in the bowl; the temperature should be between 140 to 160°F (60-71°C).
2. To help your dishwasher clean at peak performance make sure that no other water sources are being run at the same time as the dishwasher, e.g., shower, washing machine or outdoor sprinkler. When the water pressure drops too low, the dishwasher does not receive enough water during the filling part of the cycle, leaving your dishes only partially clean.
3. When using water to prepare foods, start with cold water. Hot water may contain higher levels of metals. The metals in water pipes and plumbing fixtures dissolve more easily in hot water.
4. Cut back on water usage by installing aerators on all faucets in your house. This little device gives the illusion that more water is coming out of the faucet when, in fact, part of the stream is air.
5. During winter months you may notice that the water in your house is cloudy. Water is often cloudy when air gets into it, creating harmless little bubbles that disappear if you allow it to sit for a few minutes. Also, soap that has not been properly rinsed out of dishes may also cause cloudy water.
6. If you are concerned about the taste, color or odor of the water in your house, have it tested. The test is not expensive and is especially important for people who drink water from a well. Testing bottles can be obtained from municipal offices or a water testing company. The best time to have water tested is in the spring, however some people test with every season. The cost of the test may be higher if it is to be done for the purpose of buying or selling a house. **Note**: Avoid shock chlorinating your well unless the test result shows this treatment is necessary.
7. Health Canada recommends that all bottled water be refrigerated. Check the bottling date and best before date on the bottle to determine how fresh the product is. Like many other food products, bottled water normally contains low numbers of harmless bacteria. However, if

stored for prolonged periods at room temperature, these bacteria can multiply rapidly. **Tip**: For maximum satisfaction from your bottled water cooler follow the instructions and clean with every bottle change.

8. To save water after every toilet flush, fill a large plastic soda bottle with sand or water and put it in the toilet tank. Avoid using a brick – it can break down and cause major plumbing problems.

9. In winter, dry skin is often a problem. **Dry Skin Solutions**: Dissolve 1 cup (250 mL) of salt in the bath water to soften and moisturize your skin. This is also an old treatment **for relaxation and for joint pains** – combine ½ cup (125 mL) each baking soda and dry milk powder and 1 cup (250 mL) each epsom salts and sea salt. Combine in an airtight container and add 3 to 4 large spoonfuls to your bath.

10. Give your family a late Christmas gift by **reducing your foot odor problem**. Take 2 tea bags and soak them in 1 cup (250 mL) of hot water for 1 hour. Add the tea solution to 3 cups (750 mL) of water (any temperature). Soak your feet for 15 minutes.

11. Make your own **breath freshener** by boiling 1 tsp. (5 mL) of cinnamon in 1½ cups (375 mL) of water. Store the mixture in a clean bottle.

12. **To remove water stains from wood**, lay a thick blotter over the spot and press it with a warm iron until the stain is gone or rub mayonnaise into the spot and leave it overnight. Remove the excess in the morning.

13. Use a hairdryer to get rid of unexpected watermarks on clothing, especially handy when you are in a hurry. **Note:** Always unplug hairdryers when they are not in use.

14. Put a handful of salt in cold water and soak clothing in it for twenty minutes before washing. This will help prevent colors from fading because the salt sets the colors.

15. To ensure that your pet has clean fresh water all day long, fill his/her bowl with ice water every morning. As the ice melts your pet will be cooled and refreshed.

15 Hints to Help Raze a Stink

1. For a nice aroma in the house, sprinkle coffee grounds onto a warm electric stove element.
2. Eliminate foul odors in the kitchen by baking an orange at 325°F (160°C) for 10 minutes.
3. Leave a dish of vinegar in a room to keep the area smelling fresh. This works well for cars or cottages that are not being used regularly. It also works on tobacco odors.
4. For cupboards that have been newly painted, leave an onion in the cupboard to get rid of paint fumes. Also, set out a plate of salt to mask new paint smell in a room.
5. Fill old pantyhose with crumpled newspaper and suspend them from your basement ceiling to fight a damp, musty smell.
6. Stuff newspaper into shoes or boots to get rid of foul odors. This technique also works well for luggage that has not been used for a long period of time. Also, sprinkle baking soda in sneakers.
7. **Fish smell on fingers**: Sprinkle powdered mustard on fingers, then add enough lemon juice to make a paste; rub in well then wash with soap and water. **Fish smell in the air**: After cooking fish. Place a pierced lemon in a 300°F (150°C) oven for 15 minutes. Leave the door slightly open.
8. **Onion smell on hands**: Rinse hands with vinegar.
9. Freshen a lunchbox by moistening a piece of bread with vinegar and leaving it in the lunchbox.
10. To remove odors on a cutting board, scrub with a paste of baking soda and water. Let sit, then wipe with a cloth or sponge.
11. Save the rinds of squeezed lemons in a bag or container in the freezer. To prevent the kitchen from smelling, grind up lemon rinds in the garburetor.
12. **Avoid bad breath:** Chew parsley after eating. Also, keep your teeth brushed and flossed. Another solution is to rinse with 1 tsp. (5 mL) baking soda in ½ cup (125 mL) of water after each meal.

13. Keep a bowl of baking soda inside your microwave to prevent food odors from taking over. Remove it before using the microwave.

14. Put a couple of mothballs between the garbage can and the plastic garbage bag liner so that you won't smell the garbage.

15. **Perspiration odor**: Sometimes even after you launder your clothing it still smells. What it needs is a good wash and rinse, then a soaking in vinegar to help it smell clean. Or add a little vinegar to the rinse water when washing wool skirts or sweaters.

15 Ways to use Baking Soda

1. Gargle with baking soda and water to soothe a sore throat.
2. Use baking soda as a substitute for toothpaste.
3. To kill germs, soak your toothbrush in water and baking soda following a cold or flu.
4. For bug bites, mix baking soda with a small amount of water. Apply the paste to the bites.
5. If you burn the inside of a cooking pot, sprinkle the pot with baking soda and fill half full with water. Place the pot on the stove and let the water boil for 5 minutes to help loosen the burnt contents.
6. Cabbage will be more tender if you add ½ tsp. (2 mL) of baking soda to the cooking water.
7. Sprinkle baking soda on the fat of pork chops to help make them crispy.
8. To clean your sink drain, pour baking soda into the drain. Wait for a few minutes and then turn on the tap.
9. Pour ½ box of baking soda into your dishwasher soap dispenser to give the dishwasher a good cleaning.
10. To eliminate food odors, keep one box of baking soda in the freezer and one in the fridge.
11. Deodorize the bathroom by mixing baking soda with bath salts. Leave the combination in an attractive open container on the toilet tank or counter.
12. Sprinkle baking soda on your dog and brush him/her to remove odors.
13. You can extend the life of fresh flowers by adding baking soda to the water in the vase.
14. Use baking soda instead of fabric softener in the rinse cycle.
15. Test baking soda for freshness by pouring a few drops of vinegar onto ½ tsp. (2 mL) baking soda. If the mixture bubbles, the baking soda is still fresh.

15 Solutions for Organizing Your Kitchen

1. Place your spices, herbs and nuts in labeled plastic bags. Insert the bags into the pockets of an inexpensive clear shoe organizer and hang it up.
2. Use coiled mini photo albums to file individual category recipes.
3. To see canned goods at the back of a cupboard, adjust one or more shelves inside pantry on an angle. Fasten a wide strip of wood to the front shelf edge. Lay cans in rows; they will roll forward as used.
4. Especially in smaller kitchens, hang utensils, pots and pans and scissors from hooks or ceiling-mounted pot racks. Minimize counter clutter.
5. Store baking pans upright in the cupboard above the fridge. Using plywood, make dividers, with spacers on the cabinet top and bottom.
6. When storing plastic containers, save fewer than ten different sizes. Color code lids, containers and storage bins to match quickly.
7. Paint the inside of a mayonnaise jar white. Place your valuables inside and store in your pantry.
8. Gluing pieces of corkboard inside your cupboard doors creates an instant kitchen paper organizer for school schedules, bills, etc.
9. Short of storage – use clothespins attached to hangers to hang placemats inside a closet also fold tablecloths over hangers.
10. Save plastic muffin cup containers for twist ties, bread bag clips, fridge magnets, toothpicks and bulk spices.
11. Shape a coat hanger into a circle, untwist it at the top and slip jar rings over the hanger for storage in a pantry.
12. Cut the leg off a stirrup pant, gather the end without the stirrup and use as a hanging plastic bag holder. OR, cut a 2" (5 cm) hole in the bottom of an ice cream bucket and use as a plastic bag holder.
13. Store plastic wrap in the fridge to keep it from sticking to itself.
14. Use waxed paper from cereal boxes to store pies in the freezer.
15. Too many suds in the sink? Sprinkle bubbles with salt.

15 Food Prep and Storage Solutions

1. Keep bacon slices from curling by rinsing in cold water before cooking.
2. Avocados will ripen faster if you place them in a brown paper bag with a tomato or a banana peel. Store at room temperature.
3. To keep picnic food hot for a long time. Wrap the food in a double thickness of aluminum foil and place inside a cooler.
4. Apples will stay fresh for 4 to 6 weeks if you store them in the fridge and mist with water once a week. **Note:** One bad apple amongst the others will spoil all of them, so be sure to check them periodically.
5. Use a pizza pan with perforated holes when making pizza. The holes help the air circulate and form a crispy crust.
6. Do not throw away stale bread or bread ends, use them to make egg cups. Press the bread into muffin tins and bake until browned.
7. Grate cheese and shake it in a bag with flour. The flour will keep the cheese from sticking together.
8. Break up frozen canned juice with the help of a potato masher.
9. Create instant chocolate frosting by placing one Hershey kiss on the top of each cupcake. Melt in the oven for 1 minute.
10. For more flavor, store coffee beans and ground coffee in the freezer.
11. Keep cookies soft by putting a piece of bread in the container.
12. Place limp celery stalks in cold water to get them crisp again. Store celery by wrapping it aluminum foil before putting it into the crisper.
13. To flatten cereal bars, wet hands before pressing mixture into the pan.
14. You can reduce tearing by putting onions in the fridge or freezer for 1 hour before cutting. **Note**: Cut onions often and you should build up some resistance to the chemical that causes tearing.
15. Freeze coffee, tea and milk in ice-cube trays so that if you need to cool a hot beverage you won't dilute it by using ice cubes. Freeze leftover wine in ice-cube trays and use in recipes calling for wine.

15 Food Solutions

1. If you have added too much salt to a recipe, sprinkle sugar into the bowl or pot to reduce the salty flavor. If your soup is too salty, add a potato. Remove the potato or mash it into the soup before serving.
2. When baking potatoes, reduce cooking time by half by placing them on end in a muffin tin.
3. Add 1 tbsp. (15 mL) lemon juice to water when boiling rice to keep grains separate and white.
4. A few drops of vinegar added to the water when cooking rice or beans will not affect the flavor and will make cleanup easier.
5. If you run out of milk, substitute vanilla ice cream. This works well with waffle or pancake batter, hot cereal and coffee.
6. Using honey instead of sugar when baking cookies. It helps keep cookies moist longer.
7. Oiling cookie cutters will keep batter from sticking to them.
8. For perfectly shaped cookies, bake them in a muffin tin instead of on a cookie sheet.
9. Place the cheese grater in the freezer before use to keep cheese from sticking to it.
10. Berries will keep for several days if stored, unwashed, in a colander in the fridge.
11. To keep fresh, store asparagus stalks upright in a container of water in the fridge. Cover with a plastic bag.
12. For juicier carrots, cut off the wide end of each stem before storing.
13. Add a sponge to fridge crispers to keep vegetables crisp longer.
14. Once opened, store spaghetti sauce and cottage cheese upside down in the fridge to prevent molding.
15. After slicing onions, hold a metal object (e.g., a spoon) and place your hands under water to take the odor away.

15 More Food Ideas

1. Once oil or fat begins to smoke, it starts to break down and has an unpleasant odor and flavor. Safflower, sunflower, peanut, canola and corn oils all have high smoking points and are often used for deep-frying and sautéing. Olive oil has a lower smoking point but is high in monounsaturated fatty acids and low in polyunsaturated fatty acids, so it is a good choice, as is canola oil which also has a good balance of mono and polyunsaturated fatty acids. The most important consideration is to avoid trans fatty acids which have been shown to contribute to coronary heart disease. Check labels!
2. Slice part way through chicken breasts before cooking to reduce cooking time. To debone chicken, skin and bone while partially frozen.
3. Before slicing through a cooked roast: cool and freeze the meat. Once it is half frozen, slice and then reheat for perfectly even portions.
4. No more soggy beans. After boiling green beans, drain and place in ice water to preserve the texture.
5. If you find that a casserole is too liquid, add broken pieces of tortillas to the mixture.
6. Spread butter on bread and smooth onto corn on the cob for less dripping and an even coating.
7. Put tissue paper in the bottom of a cookie jar to keep cookies fresh.
8. Remove the green sprout (heart) from garlic cloves to make them less bitter and easier to digest. Store garlic in a cool dark place; it will last about two months. **Note**: To take away the garlic odor from a garlic masterpiece, add parsley to the dish.
9. The best way to store lettuce is to wash it and then wrap it in a paper towel. Place the lettuce in a paper bag and keep in the crisper.

10. Save money – clearance section mushrooms are still tasty. To clean mushrooms, brush them, washing only if necessary, they become clean but not soggy.
11. Flavor soups with a hint of dill. Chop fresh dill and freeze in an ice cube tray with water.
12. The day before your next party, make ice cubes and, after they are frozen, drop the ice cubes into a paper-bag. The ice cubes will not stick together. Continue freezing ice until you have as much as you need. Ice recipe is below. **Note**: To keep ice cubes from sticking to the tray, every so often spray the tray with nonstick cooking spray.
13. Avoid shuffling through coupons by writing the letter "C" beside the appropriate item on your grocery list.
14. For healthy eating, shop the outside aisles at the supermarket – meat, fruits, vegetables, dairy – the more expensive processed items are in the middle aisles.
15. To save money, plan menus around items on hand and sale items in the supermarket flyers.

Recipe for Ice: If you need a recipe for ice, maybe you should rethink throwing a party.

15 Ideas for Fruits and Veggies

1. Place unripe **avocados** in a bowl with apples, pears and/or bananas to speed up the ripening process.
2. **Sweet potatoes** have a short shelf life. Do NOT store them in the fridge; they are best stored in a cool, dry, dark place. Use within seven days.
3. When peeling **tomatoes**, use a deep-fat-fryer basket to insert and remove tomatoes from boiling water. In a pinch the same basket also doubles as a vegetable strainer. **Note:** Do not use aluminum when cooking tomatoes, the acid reaction from the tomatoes may cause an unpleasant taste. Do NOT store tomatoes in the fridge.
4. While cooking, keep the smell of **cabbage** and **cauliflower** to a minimum by adding an uncut celery stalk or half a lemon to the pot or pan.
5. **Cabbage** is delicious and nutritious and, how shall we say . . . cheap. Chop one or several heads of cabbage and freeze whatever you do not use. Toss into soups and casseroles.
6. Save the bottom of fresh **asparagus** stalks. Using a potato peeler, peel the ends until you reach the soft part. Cook as usual.
7. To cook several **winter squash** at once place them, halved and seeded, in a large roaster (cut side down). Add enough water to fill one-quarter of the roaster. Cover and bake at 350°F (180°C) until soft, approximately 50 minutes. The peel will come off easily, leaving the squash ready to mash.
8. Use potato flakes to thicken puréed **applesauce**, **squash** or **pumpkin**. The difference in flavor is unnoticeable.
9. To add flavor to **sauerkraut** during the canning process, add bay leaves to the pot while you layer the cabbage and salt. Remove the leaves before filling the jars.
10. **Preserving foods** can be a rewarding and tasty way to feed your family. According to recent studies: **Freezing**, was rated low on human effort and time required but high on cost and flavor satisfaction. **Pickling** is rated high on time and flavor satisfaction; human effort scored moderate and the dollar cost depended on the recipe.

According to the results, **canning** takes the most human effort and is moderately rated for time required, cost and flavor satisfaction. Lastly, **drying** not only requires special utensils it also takes a lot of time and money. The results for quality of flavor satisfaction were varied and human effort scored moderate.

11. Add vinegar to hard water in the water bath at **canning** time to avoid hard-water spots on sealers. **Note**: For damp storage areas, wipe the outsides of filled jars with vinegar to keep mold away.
12. While making **jam**, cut down on carbohydrates by substituting Splenda for sugar. Let the jam simmer for an additional 20 minutes after it is cooked. The cost is a little more but Splenda is a natural derivative of sugar and does not contain Aspartame.
13. To remove wax from **homemade jams**. Turn a corkscrew into the wax and then carefully pull it out.
14. Prevent **pumpkin pie** from getting a soggy crust by brushing the unbaked crust with egg white; bake for 7 minutes, or until lightly browned. Add the filling and bake according to the recipe.
15. If you have a problem eating mushy **frozen fruit** (as I do), place the fresh fruit on a cookie sheet and freeze; place in containers or freezer bags. Freeze and take out portions as needed.

15 Brown Bag Lunch Ideas

1. To liven up children's lunches cut sandwiches, cheese and meat using a variety of cookie cutters. Include a joke or message in lunches once in awhile, especially if your child needs practice learning to read.

2. Cut food costs by buying full-size boxes or bags of snack foods and putting a handful into plastic containers. Yogurt and puddings scooped from large containers into small ones will not only save money but will help you monitor how much of each food your child is eating when the reusable containers return home.
3. Keep thermos foods extra cold or hot by filling the thermos with boiling or ice-cold water and pouring it out before adding food.
4. Freeze juice boxes and use them as ice packs. When lunchtime arrives they will be cool and slushy.
5. For easier-spreading, freeze breads first before making sandwiches. Pack and freeze a variety of sandwiches for one week. Spread margarine or butter on both slices of bread to keep the sandwiches from becoming soggy. Let the frozen sandwiches thaw out just in time for lunch. Do not freeze sandwiches that have salad dressing or mayonnaise on them.
6. Add variety to plain old sandwiches, try: kaiser rolls, poppy seed buns, waffles, rice cakes, tortillas, focaccia, raisin, date or cinnamon bread, crackers, croissants, mini muffins, pita bread, bagels, hotdog or hamburger buns.

7. To prevent salads from becoming soggy, put dressing on the bottom of the bowl. Next, layer tomatoes and other vegetables and place the lettuce on top. Toss before eating.
8. Save condiments, wet wipes, napkins and straws from fast food restaurants. Use them in lunch bags.
9. Save empty film containers for medicine, money or salad dressing. Also, put a toothpaste and toothbrush in lunch bags for after-meal brushing.
10. Cut a kiwi in half and eat with a spoon or cut into bite-sized pieces and eat with a toothpick.
11. To ripen green bananas store them in a plastic bag.
12. Place apples in the crisper without washing. Do not store apples in the same drawer with carrots because apples give off ethylene gas that will make carrots taste bitter.
13. When baking cookies make a double batch of dough and freeze half for fresh cookies later on.
14. Place pieces of waxed paper between iced cookies to prevent them from sticking together.
15. Start a brown bag club at work and assign each person to make lunch for everyone in the club on different days of the week.

15 Solutions for Healthy Snacks for Kids

1. Snacks can help children get the proper nutrients and energy they need throughout the day. It is important to offer them choices of snacks that are appealing to them.
2. Let children help choose snack supplies when shopping – fruits, vegetables, cheeses, etc.
3. Have designated snack places in the cupboard and refrigerator. Keep them supplied with healthy, ready-to-eat snacks.
4. Offer snacks at designated times during the day, e.g., mid-morning, after school. Don't offer snacks just before meal times.
5. To keep portions a reasonable size, place them in individual plastic bags or containers.
6. Combine food groups to create more nutritious and filling snacks, e.g., spread apple slices or celery with peanut butter, serve whole-grain crackers or cereal with milk; spread whole-grain crackers with peanut butter or cheese.
7. **Dairy Snack Combos**: Yogurt smoothies with bananas or berries; non or low-fat yogurt or cottage cheese with fruit; string cheese with whole-grain crackers or apples; frozen yogurt with fresh berries; low-fat chocolate milk with fresh fruit.

8. **Veggie Snack Combos**: Carrot or celery sticks, cucumber rounds or broccoli trees with low-fat yogurt dip or hummus; **Ants or Ladybugs on a Log** – Spread celery stalks with peanut butter or cheese spread. Sprinkle with raisins or dried cranberries.

9. **Fruit Snack Combos**: Fresh fruit or no-sugar-added canned fruit is a great snack. Serve with a glass of milk, low-fat yogurt or whole-wheat bagels. Fruit bars, e.g., Fig Newtons are a good sweet-treat choice as are Fruit Shakes made with fruit juice or low-fat milk or yogurt.

10. Fruit juices are loaded with sugar – offer whole or sliced fruit as a healthier alternative.

11. Frozen grapes are a real treat and couldn't be easier to make. Just keep a bag of washed grapes in the freezer.

12. **Grain Snack Combos**: Whole-wheat bagels or English muffins with tomato sauce and melted cheese; air-popped popcorn and a glass of milk; baked tortilla chips with salsa; low-fat granola bars and milk or fruit; whole-grain cereal or granola with milk.

13. Nuts are loaded with protein, minerals and vitamins. They are high-fat, but it is good fat.

14. Make your own **Trail Mix** by combining peanuts, chopped almonds, or sunflower seeds, raisins, dried cranberries and low-fat granola.

15. **Tortilla Pinwheels** can be very versatile:
    - **Peanut Butter** – Spread a whole-wheat tortilla with creamy or chunky peanut butter and a bit of honey. Sprinkle with low-fat granola. Roll up and slice into bite-sized pinwheels.
    - **Banana Peanut Butter** – Spread peanut butter on a tortilla and roll around a peeled banana. Slice into pinwheels.
    - **Veggie** – Spread low-fat cream cheese on a whole-grain tortilla; sprinkle with finely chopped cucumber, broccoli, red pepper, carrots, etc. Roll up and slice into pinwheels.
    - **Turkey or Ham** – Spread low-fat cream cheese or mayonnaise on a whole-wheat tortilla; layer with turkey or ham. Sprinkle with shredded cheese and shredded lettuce. Roll up and slice into pinwheels.

15 Ways to Grill to Perfection

1. Brush or spray oil on cooking grill or warming racks to prevent food sticking to cooking surface. Or spray oil directly on food before placing it on the grill.
2. When using an acid-based marinade, be sure to use only containers made of glass, ceramic, stainless steel or food-safe plastic sealable bags. **Note:** Aluminum containers create a chemical reaction that can darken the food and the container.
3. When choosing wood fuel, choose hardwoods such as: oak, apple, olive and cherry. They are best because they burn slowly and emit a pleasant aroma.
4. Flip permanent briquettes occasionally. To clean them, ignite the grill and close the cover; burn at a high setting for 15 minutes.
5. **Be prepared** – Keep a bucket of sand and a spray water bottle on hand in case of fire.
6. **Be safe** – Never store a propane tank under or near your barbecue or in an indoor shelter. Store upright in the shade away from combustible materials.
7. Prevent food from burning by brushing on thick marinades and sauces during the last few minutes of cooking.

8. **Basic Barbecue Marinade**: Combine 1 crushed garlic clove, 3 tbsp. (45 mL) olive oil, 3 tbsp. (45 mL) dry sherry, 1 tbsp. (15 mL) Worcestershire sauce, 1 tbsp. (15 mL) soy sauce and freshly ground black pepper to taste. Stir and pour over fish or meat.

9. Before cooking always preheat barbecue for 15 minutes. An open barbecue is hot (as opposed to medium or low) when you cannot leave your hand close to the grill for more than 3 seconds.

10. This summer make it a point to experiment with grilling foods other than meat. Pizza is an example of food that has a whole new flavor when grilled. Raise the grill rack away from the fire and put a piece of foil under the pizza to prevent cooking the bottom too quickly. **Tip:** If you choose not to put foil under the pizza, brush the bottom with oil and put it oiled side down on a medium-hot grill. Cook for 6-8 minutes.

11. For protection against rust, paint your barbecue with heat-resistant enamel (available at hardware stores).

12. To barbecue corncobs wrap them in buttered foil and cook for 15-20 minutes. Or place the cobs directly on the grill with the husks left on. The husk will protect the corn from burning.

13. Wood chips add a smoky flavor to grilled food. Soak chips in water for about 1 hour so they don't burn; place your smoker box in with the barbecue and cook food as usual.

14. Avoid contamination by using 2 separate platters and utensils, 1 set for handling the raw meat and a different set for taking the meat off the grill once it is cooked.

15. **Direct Cooking versus Indirect Cooking**: Foods that take less than 25 minutes, e.g., boneless chicken breasts, pork chops and steak are grilled directly over the barbecue flame. Indirect cooking is used for foods that require longer cooking times at a lower temperature, e.g., whole birds and roasts. In this case heat is placed to the side of the food instead of directly under it.

15 Ways to Really Enjoy Chocolate

1. The good news is that chocolate contains traces of several essential nutrients such as: iron, calcium, potassium, vitamins A, C, D, E, thiamine, niacin, riboflavin and phosphorus. Recent studies have found that the flavonoids in chocolate may be helpful in guarding against heart disease. Dark chocolate is the most beneficial.
2. The not so good news is that chocolate has a high fat content. Check that the chocolate you buy contains cocoa butter rather than palm oil or extenders like soy flour.
3. Good chocolate usually contains only chocolate, sugar, cocoa butter, lecithin and vanilla.
4. White chocolate has no chocolate liquor, so it is not a true chocolate. It contains sugar, cocoa butter, milk solids, lecithin and vanilla. If the label doesn't mention cocoa butter it is not white chocolate.
5. Compare the caffeine levels between coffee and chocolate. One cup (250 mL) of coffee has 2½ to 6¼ oz. (75 to 175 g) of caffeine in a cup, cocoa has ¾ oz. (25 g) or less.
6. Dark chocolate may be kept up to 10 years if stored properly. Wrap chocolate in plastic and place it in a cool, dry, airy place.
7. Milk chocolate and white chocolate should not be stored for more than nine months because of the milk solids they contain.
8. "Bloom" is the blotchy grey-white color that chocolate may develop if stored in a warm place. If stored in damp conditions grey sugar crystals may appear on the surface. You can continue to use the chocolate for cooking and baking without the flavor being affected.
9. Chocolate that has been overheated may separate. As long as it has not been scorched it can be saved. Stir in vegetable oil (1 tbsp./15 mL oil to 6 oz./170 g chocolate) and reheat if necessary. To avoid scorching, melt chocolate in a double boiler over low heat or microwave at medium, stirring often.

10. One of the easiest desserts to prepare is a **Chocolate Fondue**. Make your own by melting chocolate with cream and a dash of vanilla or a splash of brandy or orange-flavored liqueur. Use 6 oz. (170 g) semi-sweet chocolate to ½ cup (125 mL) half 'n' half or whipping cream. If a **Peanut Butter Chocolate Fondue** is your favorite, add ⅓ cup (75 mL) smooth peanut butter and 2 tsp. (10 mL) vanilla to the warm chocolate and cream. OR, you can buy ready-made fondue at the grocery store. Following is a list of great dippers: ladyfingers, marshmallows, bananas, apples, pears, little cream puffs, strawberries, pineapple and cherries.
11. For a heavenly cake frosting and filling, make **Chocolate Ganache**. Use equal amounts of whipping cream and chocolate. Bring the cream to a boil and pour it over the finely chopped chocolate. Stir until chocolate is melted. Cool to room temperature and pour over a cake. For **Ganache Soufflé**, whip the room-temperature ganache until doubled in volume. Use as a cake filling or frosting. You may add 1 tsp. (5 mL) of rum or liqueur if you wish. For a **Chocolate glaze**, use one part cream to three parts chocolate; for **Chocolate Truffle Fillings**, use one part cream to two parts chocolate; for a light filling, use equal amounts.
12. Wear cotton gloves when handling chocolate. Using bare hands may leave imprints or, worse, melt it.
13. Make professional **chocolate curls or ruffles**. Cover the underside of a baking sheet with parchment paper. Melt chocolate and pour a thin layer onto the baking sheet. Refrigerate until cool. Slice the chocolate into wide strips. Push a metal spatula along the length of each chocolate strip. **Note:** If the chocolate splinters instead of curling, wave a blow dryer over the chocolate for a few seconds.
14. To make **chocolate leaves**, gather small to medium-sized sturdy leaves; wash and dry them. Using a fine paintbrush, smooth melted chocolate onto the underside of each leaf. Refrigerate the leaves on a baking sheet for 1 hour. Peel the leaves away.
15. To create chocolate-covered pretzels or cookies, place them on a potato masher and ease it into a melted chocolate mixture. Cool on parchment paper.

15 Clues for Choosing Wine

1. Before purchasing a bottle of wine inspect it. The bottle should not feel too hot or cold. Look at the cap to be certain that it is dry and free of wine stains. The cork should not stand above the lid of the bottle. Push down on the cork with your thumb – it must feel firm but move slightly. If the cork easily pushes down the neck do not buy the wine. If the air-space is more than 1" (2.5 cm) some leakage may have occurred. Previously a sign of inexpensive wines, plastic corks and screw caps are being used on many better wines to prevent oxidation.

2. Wine that is capped instead of corked is ready to drink when it is purchased. Wine that does not need aging can be stored standing up for a short time. Wine that needs to age should be lying on its side to keep the cork damp so that no air can reach the wine.

   Note: Wine can breathe through the cork; odors in the atmosphere may be absorbed.

3. At a restaurant, smelling the cork is not necessary. The cork smell will tell you nothing about how the wine tastes. However, the cork will be either wet or dry, which will help you determine if the wine was properly stored. A dry cork may mean evaporation through the cork and oxidation – not good!

4. The ageing period for wines varies depending on selection. A general guideline is: inexpensive wines are to be consumed at the time of sale; reserve wines are finer quality – reds are best after 2 months and before 1 year, whites are best after 1 month but before 1 year. Following these categories are high-end wines whose shelf life depends upon the individual characteristic of that particular brand.

5. The ideal temperature of a wine cellar is 50 to 53°F (10 to 12°C). The best humidity level is 75%. Humidity prevents the cork from drying out and allowing wine to evaporate. Too much humidity may encourage fungus growth.

6. All wine is best stored in the dark, away from any vibrations, such as the laundry room.

7. When purchasing wine in a restaurant you are paying for a service. In the cost of doing business it is necessary and standard to mark-up wine 2 to 3 times the price that you will see it in a retail outlet (just like most other foods).
8. When transporting wines at any time of year, wrap bottles in 1" (2.5 cm) thick newspaper for shipping. After the move allow the bottles to rest for 4 to 6 weeks before opening.
9. Match the weight of the food with the weight of the wine. Lighter foods pair with lighter wines, e.g., salad or light fish with a Pinot Grigio or Muscadet, red meats with a Cabernet Sauvignon or Burgundy.
10. When serving wine with meals, serve the wine first then follow with food. When serving more than one wine at a meal, serve a young wine before an older one, a white before a robust and a dry before a sweet wine.
11. Avoid drips when pouring wine by giving the bottle a slight twist as you finish pouring, before returning the bottle to an upright position.
12. Wine glasses should be filled only half to two-thirds full so the wine has room to swirl and release more of its aroma.
13. Cooking wines often have salt or MSG added to them to make them undrinkable. Consider using real wine for a better flavor.
14. For a variation on steamed vegetables add a few tablespoons of red or white wine to the water. In cooking, you may substitute apple, orange or pineapple juice, chicken broth, rum or brandy extracts or non-alcoholic wine or beer for wine.
15. To remove a wet red-wine stain, quickly sprinkle salt on it. Then put the item in cold water and attempt to dab out the stain before washing the fabric.

Cheers!

15 Suggestions To Keep Summer From Bugging You

1. Make your own **mosquito repellent** by combining 1 gallon (4 L) water, 4 tbsp. (60 mL) lemon dish soap and 3 tbsp. (45 mL) Original Listerine. Pour into spray bottle and apply as needed.
2. If you have an ant problem, to keep them away draw a chalk line wherever the ants like to gather. Also, you won't catch an ant sipping a cup of coffee or tea, they hate both! Lay mint-flavored tea bags in drawers and cupboards to repel ants. Replace the bags every few months. Or drop a few coffee grounds around the perimeter of your house, they won't like that either.
3. Repel slugs by wrapping a length of copper around the bottom of plant pots and stems. The copper reacts with slug slime and causes a flow of electricity.
4. Herbs are nature's insecticide. Plant a variety of them to deter bugs. For more power put onions and garlic in a jar of water. Let stand for 5 days and then spray your plants with the water.
5. Onions and garlic discourage Japanese beetles and aphids on lettuce and beans, but beans and peas grow better if kept away from onions and garlic. On the other hand, carrots and parsnips do like to be beside onions.
6. Apply soap, vinegar, toothpaste or ammonia to mosquito bites to take away the itch. The product After Bite is effective, however, After Bite for Kids does not sting and also works.

7. Plant radishes near cabbage to repel maggots. Also, plant lettuce beside cabbage, the lettuce will deter the cabbage moth, when the moth flies over the cabbage to lay eggs it will think the cabbages are lettuce and keep flying. Plant cabbage, cauliflower and broccoli beside sage, mint, oregano or parsley plants but not near tomatoes.
8. A chigger is a mite that causes intensely irritating itches. Apply Preparation H to a chigger bite.
9. To get rid of fleas in the carpet sprinkle Borax over the area and let stand for 24 hours before vacuuming.
10. Apply WD-40 to take away the itch of a horsefly bite.
11. Put meat tenderizer or mud on bee stings.
12. Spices anise and coriander guard plants against aphids.
13. Plant basil, marigolds or onions near tomatoes because they repel worms, carrot and fruit flies.
14. A good **flower preservative** is to combine: 2 tbsp. (30 mL) vinegar, 2 tbsp. (30 mL) white sugar with 1 quart (1 L) of water. The sugar acts as a food and the vinegar inhibits the growth of organisms.
15. Before bringing fruits and vegetables inside from the garden, place chicken wire over a bottomless wooden box. Rinse the vegetables on top of the chicken wire to wash away bugs before carrying the food inside. **Note:** If flies are a problem and you do not want to use bug spray inside your house try hairspray. The spray will freeze their wings so they are easy to swat.

15 Top Soil Tips

1. Push a knitting needle or pencil into the soil of a houseplant. If it comes up dry, your plant needs watering.
2. Recipe for **healthy potting soil**: 2 parts good garden soil, 1 part sand and 1 part peat moss (bone meal or other fertilizer). You may need to vary the recipe depending on the character of the soil and the types of plants you wish to grow.
3. Mow the lawn at least twice before applying fertilizer after the beginning surge of new growth. The first cut of the season should be shorter than usual. This removes any dormant leaf tissue. Choose a slow-release nitrogen fertilizer.
4. One of the most important steps in lawn care is finding out what your soil conditions are by having your soil analyzed annually. Some nurseries offer this service free of charge. Six common soil problems are: acidity, alkalinity, chlorosis, nutrient deficiency, salinity and shallow compacted soil.
5. If you have rich, moist acid soil: Pachysandra, English Ivy, Myrtle/Periwinkle and Ajunga are excellent ground covers. For those who have a tendency to mow over plants, purchase a Euonymous/Winter Creeper, it is good for sunny and shady sites (set the mower blade on high).
6. Peat moss can greatly improve soil conditions. It contains no nutrients but does make the soil more acidic. **Tip:** Dampen peat moss before using it to increase volume.
7. Be careful not to add lime to your lawn if grass is growing well. It raises the pH (potential hydrogen) level causing major damage.
8. You should not dig soil when it is wet because it will bake and compact to form brick-like clumps, driving out the air. **Tip:** Moisture readiness test: Make a ball of soil with your hands and toss it 10" (25 cm) from where you are standing. If the ball stays together it is too wet to work.

9. There are two basic groups of flower bulbs available to home gardeners. Hardy spring-blooming bulbs (which are planted in the fall) and summer-blooming bulbs (which are planted in spring and dug up in the fall to be stored in a frost-free environment for the winter). Tulips should not be planted in spring. They must be planted in autumn and go through a cooling period. When it warms up in the spring they will bloom.

10. Compost (otherwise known as really inexpensive land vitamins) can be fed to soil by spreading 1-3" (2.5-8 cm) of compost on the garden; till or plough into existing soil. Also, gently rake ½-1" (1.3-2.5 cm) compost into the lawn or blend some with potting soil mix.

11. Use compost to cover exposed topsoil in the fall to protect it. In the spring plough over the areas as normal.

12. Water houseplants with room-temperature water to prevent shocking the plants. **Hint:** Tap water should stand for one day to get rid of the chlorine. By doing this you will cut down on brown-tipped leaves.

13. When watering your lawn, don't over or under water, 1" (2.5 cm) of water per week is the ideal amount for most soils.

14. **Drip Irrigation**: The challenge of growing plants on or around a deck or patio is that they are difficult to reach for watering. Using flexible ½" (1.3 cm) and ¼" (6.3 mm) plastic tubing and micro spray heads, you can install a water system in about 2 hours and it will cost you under $100.00 (for an average-sized area). Check out books in stores and libraries to learn details about installing your own watering system.

15. If the soil on your land is poor quality you may want to consider building a **raised bed**:
    - Choose your garden spot and dig down 6" (15 cm).
    - Make a wooden frame around the bed.
    - Fill in the bed with a mixture of topsoil and manure.
    - Plant and water.

15 Ways to Get Your Garden Set for Autumn

1. Sprinkle moth crystals while planting new bulbs to keep chipmunks or field mice from eating them. The crystals last long enough before evaporating to keep away hungry rodents. By winter the soil will have compacted around the bulbs, which will keep rodents from digging for them.
2. Before repotting plants in the fall use a clean sponge as drainage material. Cut it to fit the bottom of the container and slide it into place. The sponge will keep the water near the roots and allow excess water to drain away.
3. Fall is the time to collect seeds from your flower and vegetable gardens. Dry them in the sun and then put them in plastic bags. Label and seal bags and store them in the freezer until spring.
4. For evergreen shrubs that bend over from the weight of snow, try winding fishing line from the bottom to the top of the bush, then tie it. The line isn't noticeable unless you are up close and it will keep your shrubs standing tall.
5. Run a power mover over fall leaves to chop them up and turn them into excellent inexpensive mulch for flowerbeds.
6. Lay several sheets of newspaper in your garden as a biodegradable mulch and weed stopper. Anchor the newspaper with soil or rocks. Avoid using newspaper pages that have colored ink.
7. Fungi, viruses and insects live in garden debris through the winter months. Rake and remove all debris from the garden and burn or compost it.
8. Harvest turnips, parsnips, Brussels sprouts, cabbage and kale after the first frost, the cold will give them a better flavor.

9. The best time to harvest pumpkins, winter squash and gourds is when the stems begin to dry out.
10. Don't throw out excess vegetables such as zucchini, carrots, pumpkins and squash. Bake them into homemade fruit breads that can be frozen or donate them to the local food bank or a shelter.
11. To ripen green tomatoes, wrap them individually in newspaper and place in a cool dark place.
12. Plant a cover crop such as winter rye in your vegetable garden. This will prevent soil erosion over the winter. Till the cover crop in the spring to enhance the soil.
13. If you are working outside on a cold day and need to do a job that prevents you from wearing gloves, rub baby oil or beeswax on your hands, your pores will close making your hands warmer.
14. Instead of selling an old baby stroller or child's wagon use it as a substitute for a wheelbarrow.
15. Following is a list of plants that have sensitive roots and do not transplant well: balloon flower, celosia, poppies, portulaca, lupins, sweet peas, cornflowers, borage, burnet, caraway, chervil, coriander and dill.

15 Secrets for Successful Indoor Gardening

Indoor gardening provides benefits beyond beauty – many plants improve air quality. Some of the green plants, e.g., spider plants, ivy, mother-in-law's tongue and bamboo plants, absorb toxins from the air.

1. Plants beautify any house. A plant that flourishes in the bathroom will likely do well anywhere in the house. Following are three household plants that are not subject to bugs, need little water and light: Philodendron, Chinese evergreen and Dracaena.

2. Create a focal point in a sunny room by laying ceramic tile on top of a plastic sheet. Display houseplants on the tiles.

3. The kitchen window is an ideal place for growing herbs. They are convenient to have on hand and the fragrance they give off acts as an air freshener that often deters flies. For great results try: lemon grass, basil mint, bush basil, chives, mint, marjoram, parsley and thyme.

4. Grow a chamomile or peppermint plant to use in making tea. Chamomile tea is a relaxing caffeine-free bedtime drink while peppermint aids in digestion. Shred ¼ to ½ cup (60 to 125 mL) tea leaves into a teapot. Add boiling water to cover and let stand for 10 minutes.

5. Add fresh herbs at the end of a cooking period. Mint, basil and tarragon change their flavor when they are dried. Add herbs to soups and salads or tie them together and drop them into a pot of boiling broth.

6. If you have several sunny windowsills you may want to try growing vegetables in your home. Plant pole beans, cucumbers, radishes, carrots, loose-leaf lettuce and cherry tomatoes in pots or hanging baskets. Fertilize every two weeks.

7. When buying a flowering plant, choose one that has big colored buds. Resist the temptation to choose a plant with small green buds, those buds will probably never open.

8. Following is a list of the most common types of **poisonous plants**: amaryllis, azalea, dumb cane, English ivy, hydrangea, lily of the valley, lantana, oleander, philodendron, pothos and yew.

9. If your plants are not blooming this may be an indicator that the plant is not receiving enough water. If the flower buds fall off before reaching full growth try watering more often.

10. When watering hanging plants that do not have a saucer, put a plastic shower cap on the bottom of the pot to catch drips.

11. Often when people see plants in distress they assume that the problem is a lack of water, but more often the plant may be in trouble because of over watering. Only water plants when the soil has dried out but before the plant has been affected by a lack of water. If the leaves droop the plant has been left too long.

12. Except for full-sun plants, raising the level of humidity will benefit every plant in your house. Cover the soil in each pot with shells, mulch or stones to help prevent water evaporation.

13. **Feeding Plants**: Once a month dissolve unflavored gelatin in 1 cup (250 mL) of hot water; let cool and feed it to your plants. When you clean your fish bowl don't throw away the old water, instead, feed it to your plants.

14. For plants that have not been re-potted in a few years, mix equal amounts of potting soil and compost to offer the plants additional nutrients.

15. Two solutions for getting rid of aphids are to remove them with a cotton swab dipped in rubbing alcohol or spraying the plant with soapy water.

15 Solutions for Forcing Winter Bulbs

Tired of winter white? Get back to thinking green by coaxing flower bulbs.

1. The easiest bulbs to force are narcissus, amaryllis, muscari, iris reticulata, grape hyacinth and tulips. With the exception of paperwhites (see below), pot bulbs in an all-purpose potting mix as soon as possible.
2. Dig up a few lily of the valley in the fall for winter forcing. Take plump bulbs when the foliage has dried. Trim the roots; follow the general potting instructions for forced bulbs; leave in a cool dark for 8-10 weeks.
3. Paperwhites are miniature narcissi that produce bunches of fragrant, white and yellow flowers. They are traditionally considered a Christmas flower and only bloom once, for about 10 days. They are one of the easiest varieties to force because the bulbs have been pre-cooled and are ready to grow. Use a pot at least 4" (10 cm) deep and cover the bottom with pebbles. Place the bulbs in the gravel so that each is half-covered with pebbles (the bulbs should be almost touching each other). Add water to just below the bulb base. Add water every few days to keep the level constant. Place bulbs in a cool place, shoots should emerge in 6 to 7 weeks. Gradually (over 1 week) bring the pots into direct sunlight. Allow 8 weeks from planting to flowering.
4. Bare bulbs can be stored in a refrigerator for several weeks before potting. However, they will still require a rooting period after they have been potted. Store them in a paper bag with holes for ventilation.
5. You can store bulbs in the crisper but not in the same drawer that you keep ripening fruit or vegetables because the fruit and vegetables give off ethylene gas that can harm the bulbs.
6. Use any clean well-drained container, as long as it is twice as deep as the bulbs you are planting. Loosely fill the pots with soil, gently add the bulbs so the tips (noses) are rim level; the noses of the bulbs should be visible; the soil level should be just below the rim.
7. Using plain potting soil works well. You can also add bone meal or a special fertilizer formulated for bulbs to the mixture (a "pinch" per bulb).
8. Since different bulbs require differing periods of time to root well, it is not recommended to combine a variety of bulbs in one pot. Label each pot with the name of the variety and planting date.

9. For flowering in January, plant in early September. For flowering in February, plant in early October. For flowering in March, plant in late October or early November. The exceptions are amaryllis and paper white narcissus.

10. Plant most bulbs closely together – as many as 6 or 7 in a 6" (15 cm) pot. Press the soil down and water well. Crowded flowers in this case will make a showy arrangement.

11. Put pots in a dark cool place, e.g., garage, basement fridge, cool basement. **Note:** If there is any chance that light will hit the pot, cover the bulbs with a box. Keep moist.

12. Pots are ready to put into a sunny area in the house when the roots emerge through the drainage holes in the pot. The amount of time to leave bulbs in darkness depends on the variety. You will know that they are ready when 1" (2.5 cm) of foliage is present on smaller bulbs and 3" (8 cm) on larger. Crocuses require 6 to 10 weeks, daffodils 12 to 20 weeks, hyacinths 8 to 15 weeks (they will bloom 2 to 3 weeks after being exposed to warmth and light. Fat bulbs give the best flowers. Bulbs should also be heavy for their size. Hyacinths can also be grown in water.

13. When indoor bulbs have finished flowering, cut off the flower stalks but leave the foliage, continue to water until the foliage has turned yellow. The bulbs can then be taken out of the pots and planted outdoors in the spring.

14. Unlike most bulbs, amaryllis will bloom over and over. After the bulb finishes blooming, cut off the flower stalk close to the base. Keep the plant moist and add houseplant fertilizer regularly. Stop watering and feeding in August, let the plant dry out and give the bulb a period of rest. You can put the pot in the dark for a few months or leave it where it is but do not water it. In early fall, remove the bulbs and clean off dead foliage. Re-pot in a clean container with the tip of the bulb above the soil; water and place in a cool sunny area. **Note:** Any bulb forced in water cannot be planted outside.

15. If you are giving a winter flower as a gift, dress it up by covering the soil with moss, pebbles or glass marbles. This is an ideal gift that your child can make for a teacher.

15 Ways to Decorate With Flowers

1. **Questions to ask before arranging flowers:**
   - How large is the room? What colors does the room feature?
   - From what distance will the flowers be seen?
   - Will the arrangement be seen from eye level or from below?
   - Is the arrangement meant to be one-sided or seen from all angles?
2. When displaying an assortment of flowers, use no more than four different colors. If you are mixing colors, stay within a theme, e.g., pastels, bronzes, primaries or jewel tones.
3. Use a variety of containers such as pitchers, bowls, cups, teapots and wine carafes for interesting designs.
4. Clean vases with a mixture of soap and water to avoid a buildup of bacteria that can hurt the blooms. Change vase water every four days to prevent bacterial growth.
5. Using a sharp unserrated knife or scissors, cut flower stems on a slant to expose more absorption area. Place fresh flowers in a container of warm water.
6. On flowers and greenery, remove all leaves that are below the water line. Put only bare stems in water.
7. Hand-tied bouquets are an excellent way to design a simple bunch of flowers at home. Purchase a pre-grouped package of flowers and add other flowers as needed.
8. Be cautious when refrigerating flowers. Many varieties of fruit and vegetables give off ethylene gas that can adversely affect flower life. Flowers

should not be placed near these items in the refrigerator.

9. Flowers may not always be available in the colors that you need, but they can conveniently be spray painted to suit your color scheme.

10. Flowers should be 1½ times the height of the container. The container should hold the flowers securely but not tightly.

11. Use an odd number of flowers for interest. Less can be more, make sure that each flower has a purpose in the design.

12. Utilize foliage to carry out a theme. You may also include artificial fruits, pine cones, twigs, cattails, baby's breath, rocks and moss. Cut pieces of greenery from house or garden plants to add to your arrangement or insert into the dark green floral foam. Be sure that the floral foam stays wet.

13. To achieve a focal point in an arrangement, place the largest blossoms, strongest colors and most unusual foliages low but above the edge of the container.

14. Round arrangements do not have a central focal point. The arrangement should radiate from the center of the container.

15. For longer-lasting blooms, move flowers to a cool location at night. Place the flowers in their container in a plastic bag with wet paper towels.

15 Tips to Help Make the Most of your House

1. Showcase only the things that you love. Tuck gifts that you "have to display" into less obvious places, e.g., children's rooms or downstairs rooms.
2. Instead of scattering family photos all over the house, choose a few of your favorites. Enlarge them and hang or display them together as a grouping or in a multiple frame.
3. Strive to position most of your plants together as a group. Scattering plants throughout a room tends to appear messy and disorganized.
4. Lamps varying in shape, color and size can add interest and elegance to your house. Coffee and end tables need not match. As with lamps, various sizes of tables, small trunks or mismatched finds from a flea market can easily become the focal point for any room.
5. If you choose to use area rugs in your house, set all of the furniture completely on or all the way off the rug. **Hint**: To clean small inexpensive area rugs, shake them thoroughly and pull them upside down through clean snow.
6. Decorative pillows add luxury and comfort to any space. To save money, sew them yourself using inexpensive remnants or scraps of fabric. Create patchwork or plain pillows and add buttons, tassels, fringes or beads to create a special effect.
7. Keep a collection of your favorite books neatly organized on a shelf. They will be easily accessible and also great conversation pieces.

8. One of the most common mistakes is hanging pictures and photographs too high. The basic rule is to hang pictures at eye level. **Note**: When hanging art, a large picture should not be any bigger than the furniture beneath it. A small picture should not be hung in isolation on a large wall.

9. Get rid of clutter. Invest in storage tubs and make sure that everything has a specific place. Less is more. A simply and tastefully decorated room can have a much greater impact than one that is filled with all kinds of "stuff." **Hint**: January and February are optimum times to "get organized" because storage containers are often on sale.

10. A tidy bathroom starts with neatly rolled up toilet paper. If you find that the paper often hangs down, place the roll with the paper coming off the back side rather than over the top. If that doesn't help, squeeze the roll before putting it on the holder. **Tip**: Store extra toilet paper in a clean wastebasket beside the toilet.

11. Scent areas such as bathrooms with aromas. Keep a candle in the bathroom (out of reach of children) to remind you to take time for yourself (a secret stash of chocolates couldn't hurt either).

12. Unless the color white puts you in a great mood, be bold. Select paint colors that set the tone for each of your rooms. Do not be afraid to paint the ceilings in your house. Using certain paint colors can give your room the illusion of more space.
    Note: Use a roller made for rough surfaces when painting over a stippled ceiling. To remove stipple from ceilings, wet the area with a spray bottle, hose (depending on the floor cover) or sponge before scraping with a putty knife. Eliminating stipple is a big job and may require a coat of drywall touchups before new paint can be applied.

13. The best-decorated window is usually the least-decorated window. In most cases window treatments should appear white from the exterior. Keep your windows clean. A quick fingerprint wipe will help you feel more relaxed.

14. Setting the thermometer in your living area to a temperature that you feel comfortable at can change your mood. Also, fireplaces and wood stoves can bring coziness to any room.

15. Change or expand on any of the above tips in order to make your house feel more like your home.

15 Low-Cost Effective Styling Tips

1. Before you redecorate, snap a photograph of your room. You will be able to make an impartial judgment about how to improve your living space if you take out any emotional elements.
2. Paint is the most inexpensive way to change the look of a room. However, don't limit your paint to the walls. Update any room by painting or staining your lampshades, picture frames, candlestick holders and furniture.
3. Paint kitchen chairs and recover the cushions. It is easier than you might think. All you need is fabric, a staple gun, foam and paint. Remove the old fabric from a chair and use it as a pattern for the new fabric. Remember to pull the material very tight when making your new cushion. Pre-bought slipcovers are also a quick fix for chairs and couches.
4. Choose furniture that can be used in more than one room of your home. Instead of purchasing new accent pieces, move old favorites into different rooms. Consider a dresser as a buffet table. Place a heavy mirror on top of an existing coffee table. Situate breakfast trays on the bathroom counter to organize and accentuate beautiful perfumes, canisters and lotions, to add an aesthetic and functional detail.
5. Buying furniture in sets can often eat away at a budget. Choose a style or theme for your room and buy pieces centered around that theme. Mixing in pieces that do not match the theme is often a fantastic way to add eclectic interest to the décor.
6. A coffee table can be more than just a coffee table. Options can include: wooden boxes covered with fabric, old trunks, fish tanks and groups of T.V. trays.
7. Add lots of color by using printed cushions and throws. Keep upholstery and floor colors neutral.
8. If you have an old door that you do not have a place for. Paint or stain it, or cover it with quilted fabric, and hang it horizontally behind your bed as a unique headboard.
9. Modernize a kitchen or bathroom by purchasing fresh hardware for the drawers and cabinets.

10. Instead of purchasing a brand new countertop for a damaged or outdated bathroom or kitchen, buy a piece of arborite, cut and glue it on yourself.
11. Use what you have. Look around your house for vases, fancy punch bowls, fish bowls and fill them with candies, bath soaps, interesting stones, shells, flowers or feathers (vases displayed in groups make a nice accent).
12. To create a strong statement, display your collections in groups, whether they are mirrors, photos, plants, vases, books or candles.
13. If you can't afford paintings, try framing wallpaper, dried flowers, postcards, leaves, puzzles or fabric.
14. Choose a few of your favorite photographs; have them enlarged and framed. Space them on a wall and accent each photograph with an overhead wall light.
15. Buying remnants instead of off-the-roll is an obvious cost saver but have you ever thought of buying a piece of carpet and having it bound? You will have a gorgeous area rug for a fraction of the cost.

15 Solutions to Light Up Your World

1. When choosing a chandelier, the diagonal measurement in inches should equal the diagonal of the room in feet and be no more than ⅔ the width of the table. Hang chandeliers 26 to 36" (66 to 91 cm) from the top of the dining room table. Consider using a lantern in place of a chandelier.
2. The middle of a room is not usually the best place for a ceiling light fixture because it creates shadows in corners. A quick solution is to attach a longer cord and move the light.
3. Incandescent bulbs are the most common all-purpose light bulbs. They are flattering, relatively inexpensive and easy to install. However, they can be short-lived and hot to the touch.
4. For accent and track lighting halogen light bulbs are preferable. They produce a bright white light that sparkles.
5. In the kitchen, bath and family room, fluorescent lights remain popular. They are energy efficient and can last ten times longer than incandescent bulbs.
6. Pink bulbs tend to warm up a room, making the light more flattering. Blue and green bulbs are cool, creating a serene atmosphere.
7. Create a variety of moods in a bedroom, bathroom, living or kitchen by installing a dimmer switch. Installation instructions are typically included with the installation kit.
8. Scented or unscented candles used in any room can change the mood of the space. Group candles together using a variety of heights; change the colors and scents according to the season.
9. Dust your light bulbs. Dusty bulbs can reduce the efficiency of your lighting fixture by as much as 75%.

10. Lights that are situated next to an armchair or couch should be placed slightly above the seating for dramatic effect.

11. To give your room added dimension, place a sofa table behind your sofa and display two matching lamps at the same level.

12. Although you can display a variety of table lamps in a room, the tops of all table lamps should be approximately the same height. the tops of the table lamps should be no more than 1½ times the height of the table.

13. Create your own lamp. Choose a base that reflects the theme of your room: a wine bottle, birdhouse, mailbox, covered basket, candlestick. Use something opaque so the wires won't show through. Buy a lamp kit and wire the lamp yourself or ask an electrician. Also, be sure to ask the electrician if your project idea will be safe (you don't want to risk a fire).

14. When cleaning linen, cotton and hand-painted lampshades, use wallpaper cleaner. To dress up an old lamp, spray- or brush-paint the shade a fresh color. The diameter of the shade should be no wider than that of the tabletop on which the lamp is placed.

15. The security function of interior lighting is to make your house look occupied when you are not home. A basic lighting timer is a combination of an electric clock and a switch. More expensive electronic timers can be programmed for multiple settings. Some garage-door openers can control up to four modules. When the opener receives a signal, it transmits messages in the house to turn lights or radios on or off.

15 Smart Color Solutions

1. Choosing basically the same color from room to room will give your home continuity. The only exceptions are the family bedrooms and bathrooms. There you can choose a completely separate style and color scheme.
2. White is the color of calmness and purity. Too much stark white can make a room seem lacking in warmth or welcome. Off-whites are friendlier.
3. Be careful with black. Although it is the color of strength and can ground a room, too much can be overkill. Choosing at least one black piece of furniture or accent will add a strong focal point to any room.
4. Before choosing colors refer to the color wheel. **Warm colors** – red, orange and yellow – attract attention and may appear to make a room seem smaller.
5. **Cool colors** – blue and green – can make a room seem larger. Remember, it is the contrast between colors that makes a room appear larger or smaller. A room will look smaller with a variety of wall colors as opposed to one color throughout.

6. **Neutral colors** – grey, white, tan and black – help the other colors in the room stand out and are great accents.
7. A **monochromatic color scheme** is a variation of one color. To "lower" a high ceiling try painting it two or three shades darker than the walls.
8. **Complementary colors** are opposites. If you select colors for your room from the opposite sides of the color wheel you will end up with a lively room, e.g., blue/orange, red/green, purple/yellow.
9. To shorten a hallway, paint one end a darker tone than the side walls.

10. By using strong dark colors you can give your room a formal ambiance. Adding the warm glow of candles to your wall sconces or table will enhance the feeling (very popular in dining rooms).
11. Take it as a compliment if no one notices the freshly painted color on your walls. Walls are merely a canvas on which to display your beautiful possessions.

12. The artwork in your room does not need to match the color palette of your room.
13. Find the colors that harmonize and that you like, and do not be afraid to use them – one at a time. You can start by creating a feature wall with that color. Try to restrict the main colors in your room to three or less.
14. Paint is inexpensive and is changed on average every seven years. Flooring and upholstery are bigger investments and you may want to stick with neutrals.
15. Update a brick fireplace with a few coats of paint. Start by cleaning the brick (ask your hardware dealer to recommend a paint that will adhere to brick). Next, paint the brick and then decide whether or not you want to topcoat the brick with an acrylic urethane.

15 Ways to Make a Great Entrance

1. **Flooring** – Invest in a hard-wearing surface:
   - **Hardwood or floating floors** are warm and inviting, they can be laid diagonally or horizontally. However, too much water sitting on this type of flooring may damage it and cause heaving.
   - **Stone** is durable and can be purchased in slate, limestone, granite, flagstone or marble. Unglazed stone is warmer than glossy.
   - A popular flooring choice is **ceramic tile**. It is affordable and easy to keep clean. Free workshops are often available on installing ceramic tile. For people who do not own a tile cutter, you can inquire about free cuts or cutter rentals at your local hardware store.
   - **Cork** is warm, soft, durable, low maintenance and has a unique natural look. It can be stained in many color options and finished to resist staining, scratches and dirt.
   - **Linoleum** is warm, comfortable and available in many varieties. Reduce the cost by checking into purchasing remnants. Be aware of the thickness of linoleum if it is too thin it may tear.
2. Area rugs can help reduce noise in an entrance. Place plastic drycleaner bags under area rugs to hold them in place. To add variety to an entrance, change the rug to match the colors or theme of each season.
3. Add bright lights to the ceiling. Combine the ceiling light with wall sconces, lamps or lanterns to create an inviting entrance setting.
4. Make a statement by hanging unique wind chimes directly inside of the doorway. Add a tabletop water feature near your entrance.
5. People often feel that the entrance to their house or apartment feels small and cramped. Consider enlarging the look of the entrance by using the same flooring in the entrance as is used in the adjoining room(s).
6. Keep the doorway free of all clutter. Limit family members to one or two pairs of shoes near the door. Backpacks and purses may be stored in bedrooms or mounted on large wall hooks in the hall or back entrance. Assign everyone his or her own hook. Coat racks are an interesting alternative to wall hooks.

7. Allocate as much closet and storage space as possible. Tuck mittens and scarves into a storage bench by the door. Mount plastic milk crates on the wall to make individual cubbies.
8. Use a vinyl tray or, in a pinch, a baking sheet with a cookie rack inside it as a shoe rack (especially good for wet footwear).
9. If space allows, place a chest table with complementary lamps in the hallway. Inside the table store: keys, flashlight, comb, tissues, mail, shoehorn, etc.
10. Position a deep vase or basket at a corner of the entrance for umbrellas. Place a sponge at the bottom to soak up excess water. **Tip**: Instead of throwing out a broken umbrella, remove the fabric and hang the umbrella upside down on a rope or tree branch to hold wet clothes.
11. Clean all entrance windows well. They will be more attractive and let in additional light.
12. When walking into a house there is nothing quite as lovely or inviting as fresh flowers. Avoid lilies because people are often allergic to them. Alternatively, arrange silk flowers in a vase or fill a vase with interesting rocks or shells and insert a single silk orchid.
13. A clock and large decorative mirror positioned at eye level in the entry will keep you on time and keep your teeth spinach free when greeting guests.
14. Offer a glimpse into your personality by placing a large piece of artwork in the entry. Display family photos further inside your house, those should only be viewed by invited guests.
15. Calendars and corkboards are often messy and full of clutter. Instead of displaying them in a public area, secure a piece of cork to the inside of your kitchen cupboard. Hang a calendar inside an opposing cupboard door.

15 Sharp Tips To Sit On

1. There are four arm styles to consider when buying a couch:
   - **Simple Curved Arm** (sometimes referred to as Charles of London) – works well in contemporary or traditional homes.
   - **Roll Arm** – pleated and corded on the front panel for a traditional feeling.
   - **Straight Square Arm** – perfect when searching for a simple, sleek modern look.
   - **No Arm** – makes positioning easier but may not be as comfortable for everyday use.
2. When buying an expensive chair ask what type of foam was used. High-density down costs more but does not fall apart as easily as inexpensive foam.
3. When choosing fabrics for reupholstering keep in mind that solids are easier to accessorize and you will probably not tire of them as quickly. However, patterns show fewer marks and stains. Consider purchasing leather, it will last four times longer than fabric and the more it is worn the better it looks. **Tip**: Freshen up metal or wooden chair frames by lightly sanding and painting them (use rust-proof paint on metal). It is not recommended to paint fabric, even if you see decorators on TV painting cushions and couches.
4. For dining room or kitchen chairs, put 2 layers of cloth on each seat when reupholstering, if one gets soiled you can pull it up. Staple each piece onto the chair separately and add a thin layer of foam between the fabrics.
5. Dress up folding chairs and tables before company comes by making or buying slipcovers and a matching tablecloth.
6. Whether indoors or out, milk crates can be an inexpensive solution when you need extra end tables, chairs or an ottoman. Add class to the plastic furniture by getting a piece of wood and setting it on top of the upside-down crate. Next, loosely drape or staple gun an old (cut to fit) tablecloth over top. **Option**: If the crates are being used as chairs, position a 1 or 2" (2.5 or 5 cm) piece of foam on top of the wood for added comfort.

7. After washing, place slipcovers onto chairs when they are slightly damp. They will conform to the chair and fit better.

8. For even wear, flip removable cushions on chairs and couches every time you vacuum.

9. Ergonomics experts suggest that consumers should ask themselves a series of questions before purchasing an office chair:
   a) Is the seat surface of the chair an appropriate size for the user?
   b) Can the height and mid-lumbar support be adjusted?
   c) Is the front seat slope adjustable?
   d) Is the chair comfortable and is the front well rounded so that the user does not experience excess pressure on the underside of his/her legs?

10. Office chairs are often loaded with levers and buttons that never get used. Put your chair to the test, the average person should be able to figure out all of the buttons on the chair within one minute. **Tip**: Virtually all chairs are called ergonomic these days. Test them for a few hours before purchasing because most chairs feel comfortable during the first few moments.

11. To prevent chairs from scratching the floor put self-stick bunion pads on the bottoms of the legs.

12. Apply adhesive tape to the bottom of rocking chair rockers to prevent the floor from becoming scratched.

13. To fluff up carpet that has been pressed down by the legs of sofas and chairs, fill the hole with ice cubes. When the water dries the carpet will spring back up.

14. To pack chairs for moving: Remove legs (if possible). Place wing nuts or screws in a resealable plastic bag, label and tape bag to the underside of the furniture. Tuck chair cushions and pillows inside plastic bags and use them as pads or fillers in the trailer. Leave slipcovers on. Wrap arms of chairs with bubble wrap. Pad all furniture with blankets or bubble wrap. Secure padding to the furniture with tape and rope. Cover with a plastic chair cover or large sheet of plastic.

15. Nowadays potty training chairs are best if they are multifunctional. Modern seats convert to fit an adult toilet seat or can be flipped over and become a stepstool. Keep your eyes open for the new seats that play music when the child goes potty.

15 Tips for Proper Mealtime Etiquette

1. When invited to a dinner arrive no later than 15 minutes after the stated time. To avoid being rude to other guests, a hostess should wait no longer than 20 minutes to serve dinner, because of a delayed guest.
2. When arriving at a dinner party it is customary in North America to bring a small gift for the host/hostess. A few days after you have attended a dinner party sending a thank-you note is important.

3. When setting the table, the salad fork lies farthest from the plate on the left. The dinner fork is placed closest to the plate. Place a folded napkin on the far left of the forks. For a more formal dinner the napkin is placed in the middle, on the serving plate or tablecloth. The knife is placed on the right of the dinner plate (blade of knife facing inward) and put the spoon to the right of the knife. Dessert spoons and forks are placed horizontally above the plate, parallel to one another with the spoon bowl pointing left and the fork tines pointing right.
4. Serve guests' plates or serving dishes from the left and remove empty plates from the right.
5. Do not begin eating until the host/hostess has taken the first bite, unless specifically request to, "Please start eating, before the food gets cold."
6. Cut only one or two bites of your food at one time.

7. Chew with your mouth closed. If you get food stuck in your teeth it is not acceptable to use a toothpick or your fingers to remove the item. Excuse yourself and head for the bathroom.

8. Stretching to get a dish is only correct when it does not involve reaching across your neighbor or leaning far across the table yourself.

9. If you need to leave the table during a mealtime, place your napkin across your chair. When you are finished the entire meal, lay the napkin to the left of your plate.

10. Remove the spoon from your coffee cup or soup bowl when you are finished using it for stirring or eating. Place it on the saucer or serving plate.

11. Never put elbows on the table during a meal. Once the dishes are cleared it is permissible.

12. Silence your pager or cell phone at the table.

13. Avoid playing with your hair or jewelry at the table.

14. When you are finished the main course the knife and fork are to be placed diagonally beside each other on the dinner plate from upper left to lower right. Do not announce that you are "stuffed." Do not push your plate or bowl away and lean back in your chair.

15. If guests won't leave, perfect etiquette is to remain cheerful and be patient. However, if you are desperate for them to go, start tidying up.

15 Ideas for "Entertaining" Table Presentations

1. Lighting is key when entertaining. Restaurants use three different lighting levels. Fully on during the day, dimmed for dinner and dimmed further after 8:00 p.m.
2. When purchasing flatware note that collections range from low-end to high-end, e.g., within the stainless steel category there is a vast difference in pricing and quality. Stainless steel means that it stains less than other kinds of cutlery. However, stains may still occur if they are left with high acidic foods on them too long.
3. For a traditional table setting everything should match. A contemporary table can become more interesting because you can mix and match colors, designs and shapes.
4. For formal dinners, use a white tablecloth. It gives a table more grace and ambiance than any other color. For more casual dinners, make an old tablecloth look new by draping a sheer piece of fabric on top of it or by using colored placemats.

5. Investing in good-quality white napkins is a smart choice because they can be bleached. For an informal party, arrange napkins inside wine glasses or simply drape them along the edge of the table, half on and half off.
6. For fancier gatherings, place charger plates underneath dinner plates. Use silver or gold for a very formal occasion. When selecting dishes remember that white dishes go with everything, can be used for every occasion and showcase food better than any other color. Black dishes are also a good choice but not as suitable for every occasion. As you arrange the place settings make sure that the cutlery and large plates are lined up an equal distance from the edge of the table.

7. Use a centerpiece that goes with the theme of the evening. For example, if you have a nautical theme, put a ship or some sea shells on the table.

8. Fresh flowers look fabulous if they are displayed properly. Table arrangements should not block conversation across the table. You could try several small vases or use one vase per place setting.

9. Candles add ambiance to the table. The color of the candles should coordinate with the plates, linens and flowers. **Tip**: If you are in a hurry and need a centerpiece, place one or more candles above each place setting. The combination of music and candles can create a romantic mood. For a festive dinner, add food coloring to water in tall wine glasses and float a candle in each glass.

10. Use a variety of colors and textures when planning a menu. If one of the dishes you are serving is a creamed vegetable, try to choose a completely different texture and color for the other vegetables.

11. Add color to the food, e.g., for salads use reds, greens and yellows. If it doesn't look appetizing it's not going to taste appetizing.

12. Give your meal dimension and interest by layering the foods on each plate before serving. In other words, arrange chicken, potatoes and vegetables attractively, varying the height of each item.

13. If sauces have splashed or dripped onto the sides of plates, wipe the rim of dishes and plates with a cloth or paper towel.

14. Garnish the plates before serving a meal, especially if the dishes are white or off-white. For example, finish off pastas with Parmesan cheese and chopped parsley or sprinkle paprika around the plate. That little bit of red adds a lot. Spoon a layer of sautéed onions over a potato casserole or tuck slices of tomato and sprigs of parsley between rice and meat. Adding simple finishing touches to each plate will impress your guests.

15. Before a party, fill the coffee maker with water and set it on a timer so that the coffee is hot and ready at dessert time.

Dash Through the Holiday Season with Fresh Table Decorating Ideas

1. Before setting the table, sprinkle colored glitter or festive sequins over a solid-colored tablecloth. You may want to choose a theme such as black and white, green and red, or gold. In this case it is easy to accent a table with accessories from around the house. Black is bold, so use silver or white as an accent color.
2. Cut a 12" (30 cm) piece of sheer fabric to form a lengthwise runner for the center of the table. An alternative is to cut the fabric into placemat sizes and lay it under plates. Also cut wide ribbon and tie it around each chair; finish with a big bell or bow in the back.
3. Twist ribbon around a long strand of garland and lay it in an "S" shape along the center of the table. For an added touch, weave a string of battery-operated Christmas lights through the garland. Or stand a tall candle on each side of the garland inside each of the curves.
4. Fun and inexpensive placemats can be made by cutting up last years Christmas cards and arranging them as a collage on a piece of cardboard or construction paper. Laminate the placemat. Personalize by adding a photo or the name of the person for whom the placemat is intended. Christmas cards can also be made into cutlery or napkin holders. Using only the picture side of the card, fold in half, glue gun side edges and tuck cutlery or napkin inside. Decorate with lace.
5. A bolt of ribbon can go a long way. Tie ribbon around fabric napkins, stemware or cutlery; the ribbon can coordinate with ribbon used on the Christmas tree. Ornamental French horns also work as napkin holders as do pieces of wide lace – cut 20" (50 cm) of lace and sew the ends together. Weave thin ribbon through the lace and gather around each napkin. **Tip**: Decorations such as candles, bowls of ornaments, tree branches etc. are the most appealing when they are positioned in groups of 3 or more. Use caution with candles, do not position anything close to the flame. Never leave a candle unattended.
6. Put tea lights in a crystal bowl or wineglass with water; you can add food coloring for effect. It is fun to drop red or green food coloring into water for ice cubes and/or sugar for coffee. **Tip**: To color sugar; put sugar into a plastic bag. Add 2 or 3 drops of food coloring; toss well (also use colored sugar for cookies).

7. Arrange silver, green, red or white ornamental Christmas tree balls on a silver tray. Or lay a decorated Christmas wreath in the center of the table. Put three tall tapered or chunky candles of varying lengths in the center of the wreath and add some big glass ornamental balls.

8. For a fresh smell and an interesting focal point, collect 30 to 50 bay leaves. Flatten them inside a book. Arrange the leaves in a circle, with each overlapping the next. Set a group of candles inside the ring.

9. Cut tall branches from outside trees. Arrange in a vase, ceramic pot or wooden container. Make sure that the arrangement does not obstruct the view of the guests at the dining table. You could place one arrangement on each end and one in the center of a buffet table. Add silk or fresh poinsettia flowers or spray-paint some of the branches with silver and mix them into the assortment.

10. Make your own pierced tin lanterns by drilling holes in a tin can. Drill the holes in the shape of a Christmas tree, snowman or star. Spray-paint the can and tuck a tea light inside. Have pieces of thin mirror cut and position underneath the lanterns. Mirrors will add elegance to every part of the table. Lay them under plates, centerpieces or candles. For fancy feasts, charger plates are very popular.

11. Don't throw out broken greenery from an artificial Christmas tree. Randomly place sprigs along the table. Or wire pieces together to create a small circle, decorate with small flowers, berries and bells and use as napkin holders.

12. Purchase white glitter branches, tree greenery and imitation berries. Combine the three in small bunches and tie with ribbon. Place them in the center of every dinner plate.

13. Cut last years' Christmas cards into small rectangles and fold in half to make place cards. Lean the cards against individual candles, in glass holders, or position the nametags in the middle of each plate.

14. Fasten tiny glass balls or bells to each napkin or to the corners of the tablecloth. Small candy canes or tree ornaments also work well.

15. Decorate your chandelier tastefully with pine cones, ribbons, holly, garlands or sprays of artificial cranberries.

15 Solutions for Wrapping Up the Season

1. Before purchasing this year's gift wrap consider choosing an inexpensive base like brown paper or tissue paper and then adorn the wrap with fancy accessories, e.g., tassels from old pillows, strips of beautiful gift wrap fastened around the package or curled, using the edge of a scissor, tinsel, candy canes, Hershey Kisses, coins, cinnamon sticks, artificial berries, holly, dried fruit.
2. The preparation work for this project is delicious. Collect empty assorted chocolate candy boxes to use when gift wrapping books. Cut the chocolate filling chart (found inside the box) into strips and insert into the book as one or several bookmarks.
3. You can purchase remnants of lightweight fabric for just pennies. Cut the fabric into long strips and tie big bows around packages to create excitement about the thoughtful gift inside.
4. When giving food items in a cookie tin, line the bottom of the tin with cellophane. Include a copy of the recipe with the gift. Add cookie cutters, measuring spoons and sprinkle the tin with nuts, candy or chocolate chips.
5. Save empty mandarin orange boxes for easy gift wrapping and transporting. Pizza boxes work well for wrapping up large garden stepping stones, trays of baking or candies. Wrap wine bottles with flexible corkboard and tie with raffia or ribbon.
6. Instead of presenting someone with a gift certificate in an envelope, make it extra special. Carefully remove the hook top from a clear glass ball tree ornament; stuff the ball with fake snow, tinsel or sequins. Roll up a gift certificate and insert it into the ball, put the hook top back on the ornament.
7. Giving socks, gloves or a mug for Christmas? Add an extra treat by dipping a plastic spoon into melted chocolate. Hold the spoon above the chocolate so that it drips. (You may need to dip several layers.) Lay the spoon on waxed paper and let it harden, cover the chocolate with cellophane and tie a ribbon around the neck (the chocolate spoon is perfect for dipping into a hot drink). Insert the spoon inside the gift.

8. Liven things up by giving two gifts in one. Top your presents with an ornament that can be treasured and hung on the recipient's tree. Use glitter glue to write a name or message on the ornament.

9. Instead of a regular gift bow, save old light bulbs and wrap thin decorative paper napkins around them (specialty stores carry paper napkins with a variety of designs). Mod-podge the light bulbs and then, using a glue gun, fasten Christmas greenery on the neck of the covered light bulb. Attach a ribbon around the bulb for easy tree hanging.

10. Package gifts inside a Christmas stocking or Santa hat. These and many other decorative Christmas items such as tree ornaments, ribbon, candy and flowers can be found at dollar stores.

11. Trace cookie cutter shapes onto leftover Christmas paper. Cut them out and glue the colorful shapes to wrapped packages.

12. Cut leftover paint swatches into Christmas tree shapes or candy canes and use as gift cards. Or recycle old cards and cut them into little gift cards. Punch a hole in the corner of the card and thread it with a string or ribbon as an easy way of tying the card to the present. **Remember**: Most gift wrap is recyclable.

13. Scatter rose petals on the top of a plainly wrapped package. Brush mod podge onto the petals to adhere them to the box. **Note**: Mod podge (clear sealant) may be purchased at most craft stores.
    Alternative: Cut up old Christmas cards and mod-podge them to the gift wrapping; place a doily under the card for an added touch.

14. Spray adhesive glue on top of a wrapped gift. Drop glitter and sequins all over the gift wrap. Sprinkle a couple of sequins inside the gift as well.

15. When you are giving preserves in a mason jar, why not make the jar more festive and useful? Take out the plastic insert in the lid and then add some filler batting. Cover the batting with Christmas fabric and glue down the edges. Pop the newly upholstery lid back into its ring. After the preserve is finished the container can be used as a pin holder and pincushion.

15 Ideas for Better Presentation

1. Bring wrinkled gift wrap back to life by spraying the back of the paper with starch and then ironing on low heat.
2. Buy a few rolls of solid-colored glossy gift wrap after Christmas on sale. The wrap will be perfect for every occasion and it looks expensive.

3. Nothing makes a gift seem more special than if it is wrapped in velvet and topped with a single rose. Other fabrics will work well to suit various occasions. In formal situations, business gifts are generally not wrapped. However, you can show thoughtfulness in giving a bottle of wine by standing it inside a glass vase and surrounding the wine with decorative stones. Fill a watering can with seeds and small garden tools, top with a ribbon. Fill a whimsical ceramic mug with golf tees, enclose in cellophane.
4. Use a small pillowcase to wrap your gift. Tuck the gift inside and fill the pillowcase with tissue paper. On the outside tie a ribbon, a soother, a garter or a photograph depending on the occasion.
5. If you don't want the receiver to guess what is inside the package you are giving, put the present into a small box, place the small box into a larger one and surround it with jellybeans, nuts or shells.

6. Instead of using Styrofoam as packing material for a mailing gift try popcorn or crushed newspaper.
7. Wrap gifts to set the stage for what is inside the package. Use sheet music, towels, scarves, brown paper bags, newspaper or a map.
8. Send homemade cookies to kids away from home by wrapping them tightly in a tube potato chip container. If you bake the cookies in a muffin tin they will be just the right size.
9. If you need to mail a document, a watercolor or drawing to someone, wrap the papers around the tube from aluminum foil or waxed paper. Put the tube into the original box, wrap and send.
10. To tie a package really tightly before mailing, moisten the string before tying.
11. Substitutes for store-bought gift bows: pom-poms, stickers, balloons, pine cones, silk flowers, rolls of candy, toy cars, wooden spoons, pennies, photo frames, candles, photos or postcards.
12. Cut up old greeting cards to make gift tags or create personalized labels using the computer.
13. To avoid confusion at showers, weddings, Christmas or children's birthday parties, tuck a card inside the package as well as on the outside.
14. An alternative to sending birthday money in a greeting card is to put the money inside a deflated balloon. The child will have to inflate the balloon and pop it to get the gift.
15. When purchasing gifts ask for two receipts, one with the purchase price and one without. Include the gift receipt with the gift.

15 Ideas for How to Exit the Holidays

1. Have you recently purchased an artificial Christmas tree? Before you throw out your old tree, decorations and lights . . . stop! Organizations such as shelters, Salvation Army and pregnancy crisis centers often accept these items as much appreciated donations.
2. Other than sandwiches, what can you make with leftover turkey? How about soup, potpie, turkey fettuccine, lasagne, burritos, stew, salad, pizza, tacos, stir-fry, jellied turkey loaf, croquettes, omelets and quiche?
3. When storing leftover foods, refrigerate or freeze food in covered shallow containers. Food will cool faster in containers placed on wire racks. Store leftovers within 2 hours of cooking. Discard food that has been sitting at room temperature for more than 1 hour. Do not overcrowd your fridge – leave space around containers to allow proper airflow.
4. Save leftover bread. Slice, butter and season each piece with garlic powder and/or herbs; leave it overnight in the oven with the heat off. Cut into bite-sized pieces to make croûtons for soup or salad.
5. Melt leftover chocolate to create a fondue dessert. Add candy canes for a mint flavor and enjoy on New Year's Eve.
6. Empty half-full bottles of pop or non-alcoholic punch into popsicle trays to make a cool treat. If you have leftover punch that contains vodka or gin, freeze it in an ice-cream bucket; stir every few hours to make **Slush**. It will keep in the freezer for several weeks.
7. Grate leftover lemons, grapefruits or oranges and store the zest in the freezer. It makes a wonderful flavoring for muffins, cookies and cakes.
8. If you have extra popcorn because you grew tired of stringing it onto the tree. Here is a recipe for **Popcorn Cookies**, using leftover, crushed popcorn: In a bowl, cream together ½ cup (125 mL) softened margarine and 1 cup (250 mL) sugar. Beat in 1 egg and 1 tsp. (5 mL) vanilla extract. Combine 1¼ cups (300 mL) all-purpose flour with ½ tsp. (2 mL) baking soda and a pinch of salt. Add flour mixture to margarine mixture. Stir in 2 cups (500 mL) slightly crushed popcorn, 1½ cups (375 mL) chocolate chips and ½ cup (125 mL) chopped pecans. Drop by tablespoonfuls onto a greased cookie sheet. Bake at 350°F (180°C) until golden brown, about 13 minutes. Cool.

9. When your party is over, wrap up the fresh floral table centerpiece with newspaper and gift wrap. Take it to a neighbor or lonely nursing home resident.

10. If you want to get holiday photos developed in a hurry but have unused film in the camera, snap pictures of furniture and valuables in each room of your home for insurance purposes. Now is an ideal time to take a picture of an expensive item that you received as a gift. **Tip**: Be careful to conceal empty boxes that once held valuable items such as DVD players before dropping them off at the curb on garbage day.

11. If your Christmas tablecloth has a stain on it that you cannot remove, cut the cloth into a large circle, cut a slit from the edge to the center of the circle. Hem and use as next year's tree skirt. **Note:** If you do not want to hem the edge (hemming a circle can be difficult) glue on ribbon or bias tape.

12. Instead of storing gift wrap in the corner of your basement, use some of the heavier leftover paper as shelf lining in the kitchen and bathroom.

13. Recycle gift wrap that is wrinkled or torn – don't put it in the garbage. Or layer one piece over another to make a ball the size of a human head, top it off with a hat. Place the "head" so it can be seen from the front window to deter burglars.

14. Before cutting Christmas greeting cards into gift tags for next year. Make a list of all of the people from whom you received cards. Paperclip the list to next year's calendar on the November page. This will save you time in making your Christmas card list the following year.

15. Collect unused portions of candles and rub them along the underside of dresser drawers, cross-country skis or snowboards to help them slide. Or melt down old candles and mold them into new shapes.

Solutions

Introduction – Substitutions

Guests were on their way over and I had planned to make one large pizza to feed seven hungry people. Into one large bowl I poured flour and baking powder. Then, reaching for the yeast I noticed that the container was empty. Knowing that I had only 20 minutes until our scheduled supper, I took a chance. Quickly I added more flour and baking powder to the bowl. When the pizza was put together I slid it into the oven and held my breath. Much to my surprise, the additional quantity of baking powder caused the crust to rise and the pizza was a success. Check out the recipe on page 141.

Shortly after that I began compiling lists of other substitutions for the kitchen and for anything else that I could think of. The end result is an organized set of substitutions for hundreds of everyday challenges.

This book is designed to reduce stress. It is for everyone who cooks, cleans, gardens, has children, spends time outside, and also for people who are looking for healthy alternatives. You will discover substitutions that you never dreamed of, yet they were at your fingertips all along.

Did you know that a collection of plastic bags makes a strong leash? An empty pill bottle works well as a toothbrush travelling case? These are only two of over 500 substitutes listed in this book. Keep it near by, especially when you are in the kitchen. Enjoy tips, recipes and a long list of substitutions for cooking and baking. Keep in mind that some of the food substitutes may alter the texture or flavor of your end products but they will be delicious nonetheless. *Solutions & Substitutions* was created to simplify your life. Please enjoy!

Food Substitutions and Equivalents

- Allspice: 1 tbsp. (15 mL) = 1½ tsp. (7 mL) ground cloves and 1½ tsp. (7 mL) ground cinnamon.
- Aniseed: Substitute fennel seed or a few drops of anise extract.
- Apple Pie Spice: 1 tsp. (5 mL) = ½ tsp. (2 mL) cinnamon, ¼ tsp. (1 mL) nutmeg, ⅛ tsp. (0.5 mL) EACH allspice and ginger.
- Arrowroot: 1 tsp. (5 mL) = 1 tbsp. (15 mL) cornstarch or all-purpose flour.

- Baking Powder: 2 tbsp. (30 mL) = 1 tsp. (5 mL) cream of tartar and ½ tsp. (2 mL) baking soda.
- Banana Bread: Try substituting mashed or puréed canned peaches, pears or oranges for bananas.
- Basil: 1 tsp. (5 mL) = 1 tsp. (5 mL) oregano or thyme.
- Beans, Canned and Dried : Rinse the salt off canned beans. Dried beans are less likely to cause gas if you soak them overnight and discard the water in which they were soaked. Rinsing canned beans also helps decrease gas production.
- Beau Monde Seasoning: 1 tbsp. (15 mL) = 2 tsp. (10 mL) onion powder, 1 tsp. (5 mL) celery salt.
- Beef, Ground: 1 lb. (500 g) = 1 lb. (500 g) ground turkey or ground pork.
- Beef Stock: 1 cup (250 mL) = 1 cup (250 mL) water plus 2 tsp. (10 mL) tamari or soy sauce, or 1 beef bouillon cube or 1 tsp. (5 mL) powdered stock base.
- Bread Crumbs: Put dry cereal through a food processor to create the needed amount of breadcrumbs. You can also use bran or wheat germ.
  OR ¼ cup (60 mL) of dried bread crumbs = 1 slice of bread.
  OR crush croûtons, they will give your entrée a new flavor.
- Bulgar, Cooked: Substitute couscous or brown rice.

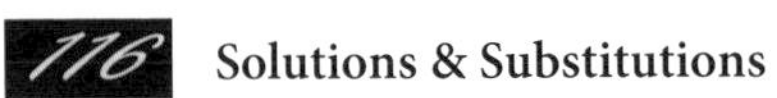

- **Butter:** 1 cup (250 mL) = 1 cup (250 mL) margarine.
  OR ⅞ cup (205 mL) lard or shortening (lard and shortening tend to brown faster than butter. Butter browns faster than hard margarine).
  OR 1 cup (250 mL) = ⅞ cup (205 mL) vegetable oil plus ½ tsp. (2 mL) salt.
- **Buttermilk:** 1 cup (250 mL) = 1 cup (250 mL) yogurt.
  OR 1 tbsp. (15 mL) vinegar or lemon juice and enough fresh milk to make 1 cup (250 mL).
  OR 1¾ tsp. (9 mL) cream of tartar plus 1 cup (250 mL) of milk.
  OR 1 cup (250 mL) curdled soymilk plus 2 tbsp. (30 mL) lemon juice.

- **Cake Mixes:** Use the same amount of club soda as you would water when using German chocolate cake mix. You will have a delicious moist cake.
- **Cake Pans:** Grease pans with shortening instead of butter, the cake will be less likely to stick to the pan.
- **Capers:** Substitute green olives.
- **Cardamom:** Substitute ground ginger or cinnamon.
- **Carob Powder:** 1 tbsp. (15 mL) = 1 tbsp. (15 mL) cocoa powder.
- **Celery:** 1 cup (250 mL) = 1 cup (250 mL) finely chopped cabbage sprinkled with celery salt.
  OR ½ cup (125 mL) = ½ cup (125 mL) chopped green peppers.
- **Champagne:** ¼ cup (60 mL) = ¼ cup (60 mL) white or rosé wine or ginger ale, sparkling apple cider, white grape or cranberry juices.
- **Cheese, Cheddar, Sharp (or old):** 1 cup (250 mL) = 1 cup (250 mL) Cheddar (medium or mild), ⅛ tsp. (0.5 mL) mustard, ¼ tsp. (1 mL) Worcestershire sauce.
- **Cheese, Chèvre:** Substitute cream cheese mashed with fresh lemon juice or feta cheese to taste.
- **Cheese, Cottage:** Substitute ricotta or farmer cheese.
- **Cheese, Cream:** Substitute equal parts ricotta and plain yogurt
  OR 8 oz. (250 g) cottage cheese blended with ¼ cup (60 mL) butter or margarine.
- **Cheese, Goat:** Substitute feta cheese.

- **Cheese, Haloumi**: This Eastern Mediterranean semi-hard white cheese has mint leaves incorporated into it. Use an equal amount of feta cheese.
- **Cheese Mascarpone**: (typically used to make desserts, e.g., tiramisu, or served with fresh fruit) 2½ cups (625 mL) = 16 oz. (500 g) cream cheese, ⅓ cup (75 mL) sour cream, ¼ cup (60 mL) whipping cream. Beat until fluffy.
  OR 1 cup (250 mL) = ¾ cup (175 mL) cream cheese beaten with ¼ cup (60 mL) whipping cream.
  OR use 1 cup (250 mL) crème fraîche.
- **Cheese, Parmigiano Reggianno**: Substitute Romano.
- **Cheese, Ricotta**: Substitute dry cottage cheese.
- **Chervil**: 1 tsp. (5 mL) = 1 tsp. (5 mL) tarragon, parsley, fennel seed or aniseed.
- **Chicken**: Cubed veal, pork or tuna fish provide a slightly different flavor but can be substituted in most recipes.
- **Chicken Stock**: 1 cup (250 mL) = 1 cup (250 mL) boiling water plus 1 chicken bouillon cube or 1 tsp. (5 mL) powdered stock base.
- **Chili Powder**: Substitute hot pepper sauce plus cumin and oregano to taste **OR** 1 tbsp. (15 mL) = 2 tsp. (10 mL) cumin, 1 tsp. (5 mL) EACH cayenne and oregano, ½ tsp. (2 mL) garlic powder.
- **Chili Sauce**: 1 cup (250 mL) = 1 cup (250 mL) tomato sauce, ¼ cup (60 mL) brown sugar, 2 tbsp. (30 mL) vinegar, ¼ tsp. (1 mL) cinnamon, dash EACH cloves and allspice.
- **Chives**: Substitute green onion, onion or leeks.
- **Chives, Chopped**: 1 tbsp. (15 mL) fresh = 1 tsp. (5 mL) freeze-dried chives or 1 tbsp. (15 mL) chopped green onion tops.
- **Chocolate Baking Square**: 1 square = 3 tbsp. (45 mL) cocoa and 1 tbsp. (15 mL) shortening.
- **Chocolate Chips**: ½ cup (125 mL) = 3 oz. semisweet chocolate.
- **Chocolate Frosting**: Melt chocolate chips on top of a warm cake. **OR** combine sweetened condensed milk with cocoa until the desired frosting consistency is reached.

- **Chocolate, unsweetened:** 1 square, 1 oz. (30 g) = 3 tbsp. (45 mL) cocoa and 1 tbsp. (15 mL) butter.
- **Cilantro:** Substitute flat-leaf parsley.
- **Cinnamon:** 1 tsp. (5 mL) = ¼ tsp. (1 mL) nutmeg or allspice.
- **Cloves:** Substitute allspice, nutmeg or cinnamon.
- **Cocoa:** ¼ cup (60 mL) = 1 square, 1 oz. (30 g) chocolate – decrease fat in recipe by ½ tbsp. (7 mL).
- **Coconut Cream:** Substitute whipped cream.
- **Cocktail 1 Shrimp/Seafood:** 1¼ cups (300 mL) = 1 cup (250 mL) ketchup, 3 tbsp. (45 mL) horseradish, 1 tbsp. (15 mL) lemon juice, 2 tsp. (10 mL) Worcestershire sauce.
- **Coffee:** ½ cup (125 mL) strong brewed coffee = 1 tsp. (5 mL) instant coffee in ½ cup (125 mL) water.
- **Coffee Creamer:** A spoonful of condensed milk will give you cream and sugar all in one.
- **Cornmeal, Self-Rising:** ⅞ cup (205 mL) cornmeal, 1½ tbsp. (22 mL) baking powder and ½ tsp. (2 mL) salt.
- **Cornstarch:** 1 cup (250 mL) = 2 cups (500 mL) all-purpose flour.
  OR 2 cups (500 mL) granular tapioca.
- **Cream Cheese:** 1 cup (250 mL) = 1 cup (250 mL) cottage cheese puréed until smooth. Add ¼ cup (60 mL) butter or margarine. Blend well.
- **Cream, Half and Half:** 1 cup (250 mL) = ⅞ cup (205 mL) milk and 3 tbsp. (45 mL) butter.
  OR 1 cup (250 mL) evaporated milk.
  OR ½ cup (125 mL) EACH coffee cream and whole milk.
- **Cream, Heavy:** For cooking or baking, 1 cup (250 mL) = ¾ cup (175 mL) milk and ⅓ cup (75 mL) butter.
- **Cream, Light:** 1 cup (250 mL) = ½ cup (125 mL) heavy cream, ½ cup (125 mL) whole milk.
  OR 1 tbsp. (15 mL) melted butter plus enough milk to make 1 cup (250 mL).
- **Cream of Tartar:** ½ tsp. (2 mL) = 1½ tsp. (7 mL) lemon juice or vinegar.

- **Cream, Sour**: 1 cup (250 mL) = ¾ cup (175 mL) sour milk or buttermilk and ⅓ cup (75 mL) butter.
  OR 1 cup (250 mL) evaporated milk and 1 tbsp. (15 mL) vinegar.
  OR 1 cup (250 mL) cottage cheese blended with 1 tbsp. (15 mL) lemon juice and ⅓ cup (75 mL) buttermilk.
  OR 1 cup (250 mL) plain yogurt.
- **Cream, Whipping:** Whip evaporated milk instead of cream. Place a 13½ oz. (385 g) can of evaporated milk in the freezer until it is partially frozen. Pour the contents into a cold bowl. Add 1 tbsp. (15 mL) of lemon juice or vanilla to the evaporated milk. Beat on high speed until stiff.
  OR Purée a banana. Whip with a beaten egg white. Add vanilla and sugar to taste.
  OR Add melted marshmallows to the white of an egg. Beat until stiff.
  OR Use vanilla-flavored non-fat yogurt.
- **Crème Fraîche**: 1 cup (250 mL) = 1 cup (250 mL) sour cream.
  OR ½ cup (125 mL) EACH sour cream and whipping cream.
  OR Make your own by combining 1 cup (250 mL) whipping cream plus 2 tbsp. (30 mL) buttermilk in a glass container. Cover; let stand at room temperature until very thick, about 8 hours or overnight. Stir well, cover and refrigerate for up to a week.
- **Crumb Crusts**: Substitute gingersnap or chocolate wafer crumbs for graham wafer crumbs in crumb crust recipes.
  Vary the flavors to suit the pie filling.

- **Cucumbers**: Chop zucchini or broccoli stems and add them to a salad.
- **Cumin**: 1 tsp. (5 mL) = 1 tsp. (5 mL) chili powder or dried fennel.
- **Currants**: 1 cup (250 mL) = 1 cup (250 mL) raisins or dried cranberries.

D

- **Dill Seed**: 1 tsp. (5 mL) = 1 tsp. (5 mL) celery seed.

- **Eggplant:** Measure out the same amount of zucchini or portobello mushrooms.
- **Eggs:** If you are short 1 egg in a recipe use ½ tsp. (2 mL) baking powder for each egg required.
  OR 2 egg yolks plus 1 tbsp. (15 mL) water = 1 whole egg.
  OR 1 tsp. (5 mL) cornstarch and 1 tsp. (5 mL) vinegar, the liquid should be increased by 3 tbsp. (45 mL) – use this substitution for 1 egg only.
  OR 1 egg = 2 tbsp. (30 mL) mayonnaise.
  OR 2 egg whites = 1 whole egg. For a better texture, add 1 tsp. (5 mL) vegetable oil for each egg omitted.
- **Eggs:** To make eggs go further when making a scrambled egg dish, add breadcrumbs – they also enhance the flavor.

- **Fines Herbs:** Combine equal amounts of dried thyme, oregano, sage and rosemary.
  OR 3 parts parsley flakes, 2 parts EACH dried chervil and chives, 1 part dried tarragon.
- **Five Spice Powder:** 5 tsp. (25 mL) = 1 tsp. (5 mL) EACH ground anise, fennel, cloves, cinnamon and pepper.
- **Flour, All-Purpose:** 1 cup (250 mL) = 1½ cups (375 mL) fine breadcrumbs.
  OR 1 cup plus 2 tbsp. (280 mL) cake or pastry flour.
  OR ⅞ cup (205 mL) rice flour (do not replace all of the flour with rice flour).
  OR flour for thickening: 1 tbsp. (15 mL) = 1½ tsp. (7 mL) cornstarch or arrowroot, potato or rice starch or 1 tbsp. (15 mL) granular tapioca.
- **Flour, Cake:** 1 cup (250 mL) = 1 cup (250 mL) all-purpose flour minus 2 tbsp. (30 mL).
- **Flour, Self-Rising:** 1 cup (250 mL) = 1 cup (8 g/250 mL) all-purpose flour, 1½ tsp. (7 mL) baking powder and ½ tsp. (2 mL) salt.

- **Flour, Whole-Wheat:** 1 cup (250 mL) = ⅝ cup (148 mL) potato flour.
  OR ⅞ cup (205 mL) all-purpose flour plus 2 tbsp. (30 mL) wheat germ.
  OR 1 cup (250 mL) graham flour.
  OR ¾ cup (175 mL) = 1 cup (250 mL) white flour. Add 1 tbsp. (15 mL) of liquid for cakes.
  As a general rule, in a recipe, you may substitute whole-wheat flour for ¼ to ½ of the amount of the all-purpose flour.
- **Food Coloring:** Add unsweetened flavored drink mix to icing (confectioner's) sugar.

- **Garlic Clove:** 1 small clove = ⅛ tsp. (0.5 mL) garlic powder OR ½-1 tsp. (2-5 mL) garlic salt.
- **Ginger:** 1 tbsp. (15 mL) minced fresh = ⅛ tsp. (0.5 mL) powdered ginger; 1 tbsp. (15 mL) grated fresh = 1 tsp. (5 mL) powdered ginger.
- **Ginger, Powdered:** Substitute allspice, nutmeg, mace or cinnamon.
- **Graham Wafer Crumbs:** 1 cup (250 mL) = 1 cup (250 mL) crushed ice cream cone crumbs.
- **Gravy:** Thin cream of mushroom soup with chicken or beef broth.
  OR Add water reserved from boiling potatoes to pan juices to make delicious gravy.

- **Herbs:** See individual herb listings.
- **Herbs, Dried:** 1 tsp. (5 mL) = 1 tbsp. (15 mL) chopped fresh herbs.
- **Honey:** 1 cup (250 mL) = 1 cup (250 mL) of molasses or corn syrup.
  OR 1¼ cups (300 mL) of sugar and ¼ cup (60 mL) water or other liquid called for in the recipe.
  OR ¾ cup (175 mL) maple syrup or light or dark corn syrup plus ½ cup (125 mL) white sugar.
- **Hot Dogs:** Substitute turkey, chicken or veggie dogs.
- **Hot Pepper Sauce:** A few drops = a dash of cayenne or red pepper flakes.

- **Ice Cream**: Substitute frozen yogurt or soy yogurt.
- **Italian Seasoning**: Combine equal amounts of basil, oregano, rosemary, marjoram, sage and thyme.

- **Ketchup**: Make your own by combining, ½ cup (125 mL) sugar, 2 tbsp. (30 mL) white vinegar and 8 oz. (250 mL) can of tomato sauce. Keep refrigerated.

L

- **Lamb**: Substitute pork or poultry.
- **Lemon**: 1 = ¼ cup (60 mL) lemon juice. Substitute equal amount of lime juice or ½ amount of vinegar (don't use for sweets).
- **Lemon Juice in Salad Dressing**: Replace with half the amount of white vinegar or the same amount of rice wine vinegar.
- **Lettuce**: A less expensive alternative to lettuce is cabbage. It is also more nutritious and keeps longer.
- **Lunch Meats**: Substitute extra-firm flavored tofu or water-packed tuna.

- **Mace**: Substitute allspice, nutmeg, ginger or cinnamon.
- **Maple Syrup**: 2 cups (500 mL) = 2 cups (250 mL) sugar and 1 cup (250 mL) water, combine and boil until sugar is dissolved. Add ½ tsp. (2 mL) maple extract.
- **Margarine**: Substitute olive oil.
- **Marinade, Meat**: Pour Italian dressing over meat for a quick and easy marinade.

- **Marjoram**: Substitute basil, thyme or savory.
- **Mascarpone**: See Cheese, Marscarpone.
- **Mayonnaise**: 1 cup (250 mL) = 1 cup (250 mL) sour cream or puréed cottage cheese.
  OR 1 cup (250 mL) = 1 cup (250 mL) salad dressing.
- **Milk**: 2 cups (500 mL) = 1¼ lbs. (625 g) zucchini. Peel then liquefy.
  OR Keep a box of powdered milk in the kitchen for cooking and baking emergencies.
  OR Combine evaporated milk with non-fat powdered milk.
- **Milk Substitutes for Kosher Baking**: Replace milk with equal amounts of rice milk, almond milk, soy milk or tea. Remember to use vegetable shortening or margarine to replace butter.
- **Milk, Sour**: 1 cup (250 mL) = 1 cup (250 mL) milk plus 1 tbsp. (15 mL) vinegar or lemon juice. Let stand for 5 minutes.
- **Milk, Sweetened Condensed**: Using a blender, mix ¼ cup (60 mL) hot water and ¾ cup (175 mL) sugar. Slowly add 1¼ cups (300 mL) dry skim milk powder. Refrigerate for 24 hours before use. It will keep in the fridge for 1 week.
  OR Combine ¾ cup (175 mL) sugar, 3 tbsp. (45 mL) butter or margarine and 1 cup (250 mL) powdered skim milk in a blender. Pour in ⅓ cup (75 mL) boiling water and blend until smooth. Yield is 1¼ cups (300 mL).
- **Mint**: Substitute basil, marjoram or rosemary.
- **Molasses**: 1 cup (250 mL) = 1 cup (250 mL) honey, dark corn syrup or maple syrup.
- **Mushrooms**: Use the same amount of cooked diced celery
  OR canned drained mushrooms: 6 oz. (170 g) can = ½ lb. (8 oz./250 g) of fresh.
  OR 1 lb. (250 g) fresh = 3 oz. (85 g) dried mushrooms plus 1½ cups (375 mL) water.
- **Mustard, Dry**: 1 tsp. (5 mL) = 1 tbsp. (15 mL) prepared.

N

- **Nutmeg:** Substitute cinnamon, mace or ginger.
- **Nuts:** Brown rolled oats (oatmeal) in a small amount of water in a skillet and use them to replace nuts in a recipe.
- **Nuts, Chopped:** When making chocolate brownies you can substitute coarse bran for the nuts.
- **Nuts and Seeds:** Substitute popcorn and pretzels.

- **Oatmeal:** You may replace ⅓ of the all-purpose flour in bread, muffin and cookie recipes with oatmeal.
- **Oats, Large Rolled:** 1 cup (250 mL) = 1 cup (250 mL) quick-cooking rolled oats. 1 lb. (500 g) = 5 cups (1.25 L) uncooked; 1 cup (250 mL) uncooked = 1¾ cups (425 mL) cooked.
- **Oil, Baking:** Substitute equal amount of applesauce.
- **Oil, Cooking:** Substitute applesauce plus skim milk if trying to get a liquid. **OR** use corn syrup.
- **Oil, Cooking/Vegetable:** 1 tbsp. (15 mL) = 1 tbsp. (15 mL) mayonnaise.
- **Oil, Sesame:** 1 tbsp. (15 mL) = 1½ tsp. (7 mL) sesame seeds sautéed in ½ tsp. (2 mL) vegetable oil.
- **Olives:** Substitute pickles.
- **Onion:** 1 small = ¼ cup (60 mL) chopped, fresh onion or 1½ tsp. (7 mL) onion salt or 1 tsp. (5 mL) onion powder. Replace yellow or white onions with red onions or green spring onions, chives, leeks, shallots.
- **Onion, Chopped:** 2 tbsp. (30 mL) = 1 tbsp. (15 mL) instant minced (dehydrated) onion.
- **Orange, Medium:** 1 = 6-8 tbsp. (90-120 mL) of orange juice.
- **Orange Zest:** 1 tsp. (5 mL) grated = 2 tbsp. (30 mL) orange juice.
- **Oregano:** Substitute thyme or basil.

- **Pancake Syrup:** ½ cup (125 mL) brown sugar, 1½ cups (375 mL) water, ½ tsp. (2 mL) cornstarch, ½ tsp. (2 mL) maple flavoring. Cook until slightly thickened (stir often).
- **Parsley:** Substitute chervil or cilantro.
- **Pasta:** Macaroni – 8 oz. (250 g) = 4 cups (1 L) cooked 1 cup (250 mL) = 1¾ cups (425 mL) cooked.
  Spaghetti – 1 lb. (500 g) = 7-8 cups (1.75-2 L) cooked.
- **Pecans:** Use the same amount of crushed cornflakes.
- **Peppermint, dried:** 1 tbsp. (15 mL) = ¼ cup (60 mL) fresh mint.
- **Peppers, Green:** Substitute red or yellow peppers.
- **Pickles:** If you run out of cucumbers, slice some zucchini and drop the slices into pickle juice.
- **Pie Crust:** Substitute graham cracker, gingersnap or chocolate wafer crumb crust.
  OR Yields 2, 9" (23 cm) pies = Combine 6½ cups (1.625 L) flour, 1 tbsp. (15 mL) salt, 2½ cups (625 mL) shortening. Mix and press into greased pie plate.
- **Pimiento:** 2 tbsp. (30 mL) chopped = 3 tbsp. (45 mL) fresh red pepper, chopped.
- **Pistachio Flavor:** Combine vanilla and almond extracts.
- **Poultry Seasoning:** 2 tsp. (10 mL) = ¾ tsp. (3 mL) crushed sage, ¼ tsp. (1 mL) EACH thyme, savory, black pepper, rosemary and marjoram.
- **Pumpkin Pie Spice:** 1 tsp. (5 mL) = ½ tsp. (2 mL) ground cinnamon, ¼ tsp. (1 mL) EACH ground ginger, nutmeg and allspice.

- **Raisins**: ½ cup (125 mL) = ½ cup (125 mL) chopped pitted prunes, dates or currants or other dried fruits, e.g., blueberries, cranberries, etc.
- **Red Pepper Flakes**: Substitute hot pepper sauce or cayenne.
- **Rice**: 3 cups (750 mL) cooked = 1 cup (250 mL) raw long-grain white rice or converted, brown or wild rice.
  OR Substitute the same amount of couscous for rice.
- **Ricotta Cheese**: 1 cup (250 mL) = 1 cup (250 mL) cottage cheese and 1 tbsp. (15 mL) skim milk.
- **Rosemary**: Substitute thyme, savory or tarragon.

- **Saffron**: Substitute turmeric for color.
- **Sage**: Substitute poultry seasoning, savory, marjoram or rosemary.
- **Salmon, Smoked**: Sprinkle canned salmon with freshly ground pepper. Squeeze a few drops of lemon juice on the fish and substitute for salmon in a recipe.
- **Salt**: Mix together garlic powder, onion powder, oregano, basil, white pepper and lemon pepper. See page 132 for herb substitutes for salt.
- **Savory**: Substitute thyme, marjoram or sage.
- **Sesame Seeds**: 1 tbsp. (15 mL) = 1 tbsp. (15 mL) finely, chopped blanched almonds.
- **Shallots**: Replace shallots with onion. The flavor is a combination of garlic and onion.
- **Sherry flavor**: Combine rose and almond extracts or use orange or pineapple juices or vanilla extract.
- **Shortening**: 1 cup (250 mL) = 1 cup (250 mL) of peanut butter for pie crusts.
- **Shortening, Melted**: 1 cup (250 mL) = 1 cup (250 mL) vegetable oil – substitute only for melted shortening.

- **Skim Milk**: 1 cup (250 mL) = ¾ cup (175 mL) water, ⅓ (75 mL) cup non-fat dry milk.
- **Spices**: See individual spice listings.
- **Spinach**: For a crunchier more flavorful substitute, try water spinach (swamp spinach), a watercress-like plant available in large supermarkets or Asian food stores. **Note**: It's listed as a noxious weed and a prohibited plant in the U.S.
- **Steak Sauce**: ¼ cup (60 mL) = 4 tsp. (20 mL) soy sauce, 3 drops hot sauce, 2 tsp. (10 mL) lemon juice and 1 tsp. (5 mL) brown sugar.
- **Sugar, Brown**: ½ cup (125 mL) = ½ cup (125 mL) white granulated sugar, ½ tsp. (2 mL) maple flavoring and ½ tsp. (2 mL) molasses.
- **Sugar, Icing (Confectioner's)**: 1 cup (250 mL) = 1 cup (250 mL) of white sugar and 1 tbsp. (15 mL) cornstarch. Blend at high speed for 5 minutes.
- **Sugar in Tea**: Dissolve hard candy or lemon drops in a pot of tea. They melt quickly and give the tea a sweet flavor. A great way to soothe a cough.
- **Sugar, White Granulated**: 1 cup (250 mL) = 1 cup (250 mL) of honey and ¼ tsp. (1 mL) baking soda. Be sure to deduct 3 tbsp. (45 mL) of liquid from the recipe.
  OR 1¼ cups (300 mL) of fruit sugar.
  OR 1 cup (250 mL) of brown sugar.
- **Syrup, Corn**: 1 cup (250 mL) = 1 cup (250 mL) honey.
  OR 1 cup (250 mL) sugar dissolved in ¼ cup (60 mL) of warm water.
- **Syrup, Pancake**: 1 cup (250 mL) brown sugar and ½ cup (125 mL) of water. Bring to a boil; simmer for 15 minutes. Add 1½ tsp. (7 mL) maple flavoring (do not overcook).
  OR Add a small amount of water and a dab of butter to gently warmed jam.

- **Tabasco Sauce:** 4 drops = ¼ tsp. (1 mL) black pepper.
- **Taco Seasoning:** 1 pkg. = 4 tsp. (20 mL) minced onion, 2 tsp. (10 mL) chili powder, 2 tsp. (10 mL) salt, 1 tsp. (5 mL) garlic powder, 1 tsp. (5 mL) cornstarch, 1 tsp. (5 mL) ground cumin, 1 tsp. (5 mL) black pepper.
- **Tapioca for Thickening:** 1 tbsp. (15 mL) quick cooking for thickening = 1 tbsp. (15 mL) flour.
- **Tarragon**: Substitute chervil, fennel seed or aniseed to taste.
- **Tartar Sauce:** ½ cup (125 mL) = 6 tbsp. (90 mL) mayonnaise, 2 tbsp. (30 mL) pickle relish.
- **Teriyaki Sauce**: ¼ cup (60 mL) = 3 tbsp. (45 mL) soy sauce and 1 tbsp. (15 mL) sherry.
- **Thyme**: Substitute savory, basil, marjoram or oregano.
- **Tomatoes, Chopped:** (14 oz. can) (398 mL) = 34 fresh tomatoes.
- **Tomato Juice**: 1 cup (250 mL) = ½ cup (125 mL) tomato sauce and ½ cup (125 mL) water.
- **Tomato Paste**: 1 tbsp. (15 mL) = 1 tbsp. (15 mL) of ketchup.
- **Tomato Purée:** 1 cup (250 mL) = ½ cup (125 mL) tomato paste and ½ cup (125 mL) water.
- **Tomato Sauce**: Blend 14 oz. (398 mL) can of whole tomatoes. **OR** 1¾ cups (425 mL) of sauce = ¾ cup (175 mL) tomato paste and 1 cup (250 mL) water.
- **Tomato Soup**: 2 cups (500 mL) = 1 cup (250 mL) tomato sauce plus ¼ cup (60 mL) water.
- **Truffles:** 1 oz. (30 g) = 1 oz. (30 g) shitake mushrooms.
- **Turmeric**: 1 tsp. (5 mL) = 1 tsp. (5 mL) dry mustard.

- **Vanilla Bean:** ½ bean = 1 tbsp. (15 mL) vanilla extract.
- **Vinegar, Balsamic:** Substitute sherry or cider vinegar.
- **Vinegar, Chinese Rice:** Substitute white wine.
- **Vinegar, Red Wine:** 4 tbsp. (60 mL) = 3 tbsp. (45 mL) cider vinegar and 1 tbsp. (15 mL) red wine.
- **Vanilla, Sherry:** Substitute balsamic vinegar.
- **Vanilla, White:** Substitute lemon juice.

- **Wine, Cooking:** Use an equal amount of apple, orange or pineapple juice or use chicken broth or non-alcoholic wine or beer. Rum or brandy extracts may be added for flavor – add them to taste.
- **Wine, Dry White:** ¼ cup (60 mL) = ¼ cup (60 mL) dry vermouth. Also try chicken broth, vegetable broth, white grape juice, water, diluted white wine vinegar or ginger ale.
- **Wine, in marinade:** ½ cup (125 mL) = ½ cup (125 mL) vinegar and 1 tsp. (5 mL) sugar, ¼ cup (60 mL) water.
- **Worcestershire Sauce:** 1 tbsp. (15 mL) = 1 tbsp. (15 mL) soy sauce and a dash of hot pepper sauce.
  OR 1 tbsp. (15 mL) bottled steak sauce.

- **Yeast, active dry:** 1 tbsp. (15 mL) = ¼ oz. (8 g) pkg. active dry yeast.
- **Yeast, Compressed:** 1 cake = 2 tsp. (10 mL) active dry yeast.
- **Yeast, Instant:** 1 tbsp. (15 mL) = 1 tbsp. active dry yeast.
- **Yogurt:** 1 cup (250 mL) = 1 cup (250 mL) buttermilk.
  OR 1 cup (250 mL) milk or low-fat sour cream plus 1 tbsp. (15 mL) lemon juice.
  OR 1 cup (250 mL) cottage cheese, blended until smooth.

Equivalents and Conversions

1 lb.	apples	4 medium
1 lb.	bananas	4 medium
1 slice	bread	½-¾ cup (125-175 mL) soft breadcrumbs
4 slices	bread	1 cup (250 mL) dry breadcrumbs
1 lb.	butter	2 cups (500 mL)
¼ lb.	cheese, grated	1 cup (250 mL)
1 oz.	chocolate (1 square)	2 tbsp. (30 mL) chocolate
1 cup	cream, whipping	2 cups (500 mL) whipped
1 lb.	flour	4 cups (1 L)
1 env.	gelatin	2 tbsp. (30 mL) gelatin
1 lb.	granulated sugar	2 cups (500 mL)
1 cup	macaroni, dry	2¼ cups (550 mL) cooked
1 lb.	meat, diced	2 cups (500 mL)
1	onion, medium	½ cup (125 mL) chopped
6	potatoes, medium	4 cups (1 L) mashed
1 cup	rice, uncooked	3 cups (750 mL) cooked
1 lb.	spaghetti, raw	8 cups (2 L) cooked
1 lb.	tomatoes	4 medium
1 qt.	vegetables, frozen	3½ cups (825 mL)

Inexpensive Alternatives to Expensive Foods

Substitute pollock for crab

Substitute tofu for meat

Substitute canned juice for carton juice

Substitute cabbage for lettuce

Substitute carrots for cauliflower

Substitute mussels for shrimp

Substitute bulk items for packaged ingredients

Substitute Healthful Herbs for Salt

Basil - brings out flavor in tomato dishes

Bay leaf – enhances stews

Chives – gives soups and salads a delicious flavor

Cinnamon – for baking, desserts and drinks

Cloves – great in meat and vegetable dishes as well as soups

Cumin – for an earthy flavor in marinades, rice, chili and tomato sauces

Curry – adds heat and complex flavor to rice, chicken, fish and vegetables

Dill – use in sandwiches, salads and soups

Ginger – gives zest to meat and baking

Garlic Salt – is great in soups, stews, potatoes and rice

Marjoram – use in meat, fish and vegetable dishes

Mustard – enhances breads, salads, stews and marinades

Onion – keeps soups and casseroles from tasting bland

Paprika – is the finishing touch to potatoes, chicken and fish

Parsley – add to soups or sandwiches

Rosemary – use on meat, poultry or fish

Sage - use on meat, poultry or fish

Herbs and Spices – How to Use and Store

- Cooking herbs and spices for too long may result in bitter or too strong flavors. For soups and stews, add herbs and spices an hour or less before serving. Crush herbs before adding. Add dry spices earlier in cooking; add fresh spices and herbs toward the end of cooking.
- Try something different – use marjoram instead of oregano, savory instead of thyme, cilantro instead of parsley, anise seed instead of fennel. Combining herbs and spices allows you to create a variety of new and exciting dishes.
- Store herbs and spices in a cool, dark place in small glass or plastic airtight containers.
- If stored properly, dried herbs and ground spices will retain their flavors for a year. Whole spices may last for 3-5 years.
- To keep herbs and spices at optimum freshness, store them in tightly sealed containers in the freezer.
- To enhance spice flavors, try roasting them in a dry skillet over medium heat just before adding them to your recipe. Be careful not to burn them.
- Do not store dry herbs and spices near any humid heat source, e.g., dishwashers, stoves and microwaves. Also avoid storing dry herbs and spices inside the refrigerator due to the high humidity.
- **Harvesting Herbs**: Pick the leaves or flower buds just before they reach their peak. Harvest herbs in the early morning but never in wet or humid conditions. Collect seeds when they turn brown and brittle.
- **Drying Herbs**: Dry herbs on racks or upside down by their stems. Place herbs in a well-ventilated, dry, cool environment. Ensure that you have plenty of air space and turn every few days. An alternative method of drying is using the microwave: lay the herbs out on absorbent paper and cook on low for 3 minutes. Please check your microwave manual for warnings against drying herbs! A dehydrator is another option.

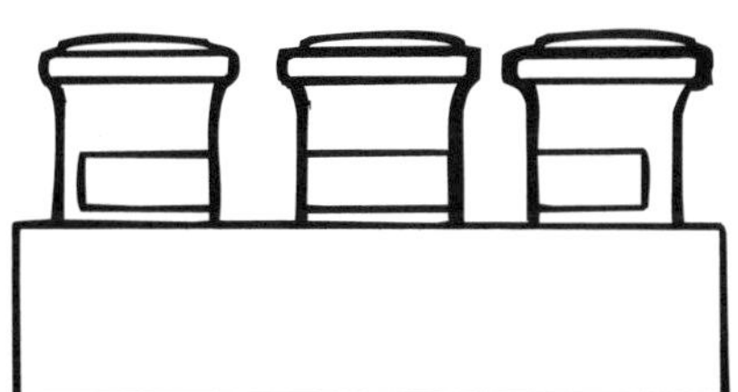

Flavoring Suggestions

- **Basil:** Bruschetta, sliced tomatoes, pesto sauce. Soups: tomato, vegetable, minestrone, chowders, potato. Vinaigrettes, green salads, tomato and egg salads. Carrots, cucumber, eggplant, beans, peas, potatoes, squash. Italian sauces, ratatouille, pasta. Soft cheese and dips, in sandwiches and wraps. Fish, beef, chicken, lamb. Flavor oils and vinegars.
- **Cilantro:** Use fresh with strong-flavored cheeses, Asian soups and salad dressings, dipping sauces, pesto, fish. Add to Asian, Mexican and curry dishes, green salads, sushi, rice dishes, salsa. Fresh fruit salads.
- **Dill:** Fish and seafood, potato salad, cucumbers, eggs, cottage cheese, sour cream, cream of tomato and split pea soup, chicken, turkey, coleslaw, mayonnaise, carrots, beets, cabbage, turnips, cauliflower, zucchini, pickles, corned beef, lamb, roast pork; baked halibut, mackerel and salmon.
- **Marjoram:** Soft and cottage cheeses, Cheddar cheese spreads, dips, onion soup, minestrone soup, spinach, green salads, asparagus, chicken, fruit, carrots, peas, beans, summer squash, tomatoes, celery, broccoli, omelets, roast beef, pork, veal, stews, meat pies, meatloaf, pot roast, ribs, shrimp, oysters, fish.
- **Mint:** Very popular in Middle Eastern and Greek cuisine. Add to peas, carrots, potatoes, eggplant, beans, beets and corn. Use in tabbouleh salad. Serve with fresh berries; add to mousses and puddings. Add to omelets, soufflés. Steep fresh or dried mint for a mint tea or add to green teas.
- **Oregano:** Cheese spreads, pizza, vegetable juice, avocado dip, cream and cottage cheese. Soups: bean, beef, vegetable, tomato, lentil, minestrone, onion, spinach. Salad dressings, seafood, green beans, mixed greens, potato and tomato salads. With peas, onions, potatoes, spinach, stewed tomatoes, mushrooms. In omelets and other egg dishes, cheese sauces, soufflés. Lamb, meatloaf, gravies and sauces, spareribs, veal, chicken, fish, shrimp and clams.
- **Rosemary:** Deviled eggs, pickles, sour cream dips. Soups: chicken, lentil, minestrone, split pea, spinach, chowders. Peas, potatoes, mushrooms, onions, celery, broccoli, cucumbers, omelets and soufflés. Lamb, beef, pork, veal, beef stew, pot roast, spareribs, chicken, sauces and gravies, salmon, baked halibut, baked sole. Use to flavor oils and vinegars.

Healthier Eating Substitutions

Use low-fat or fat-free options where possible, e.g., fat-free yogurt and sour cream, light cream cheese, etc. Also watch your sugar consumption – fresh fruit is a much better choice than fruit drinks or even fruit juices.

- BEEF, GROUND: Substitute barley for ⅓ of the ground beef or other meats in a recipe. Use soybeans in place of half of the ground beef.
- BUTTER, MARGARINE, VEGETABLE OILS, SALAD DRESSINGS AND MAYONNAISE: Use 1 cup (250 mL) of applesauce to replace 1 cup (250 mL) of butter in baking. Also try jam, honey, mustard, "light" mayonnaise and low-fat salad dressing in baking, dips or as spreads. Reduce the amount of liquid in the recipe.
- BUTTER: Replace butter or sour cream by topping baked potatoes with plain yogurt or salsa.

  SALSA – In a large pot combine:

  28 oz. (796 mL) canned tomatoes
  7½ oz. (213 mL) canned tomato sauce
  1 minced garlic clove
  1 chopped green pepper
  1 chopped red pepper
  ¼ tsp. (1 mL) dried oregano
  ½ tsp. (2 mL) pickling salt
  ½ tsp. (2 mL) dried crushed red chili peppers

  Bring to a boil. Boil for 20 minutes on low, stir occasionally until thickened. Cool. Pour into jars and seal. **Makes 3, 1 cup (250 mL) jars.**

- CANDY: Keep grapes in the freezer and pop 1 or 2 into your mouth when you have a craving.
- CHICKEN, DARK MEAT: Choose white meat. Ounce for ounce drumsticks have more than twice the fat of chicken breasts
- CHIPS AND CHEEZIES: Pretzels and air-popped popcorn are a much smarter choice.
- COCOA: ¼ cup (60 mL) = ½ cup (125 mL) chocolate "morsels" (unsweetened) cut sugar by ¼ cup (60 mL) and shortening by 1 tbsp. (15 mL). OR, since cocoa powder has more fat than carob powder, substitute 1 cup (250 mL) carob.

- **Cookies**: Snack without the guilt when you choose one of the following: Social Tea biscuits, arrowroot biscuits, gingersnap cookies, Melba toast, rice cakes, soda crackers or angel food cake.
- **Cream**: Replace cream in recipes with 1 cup (250 mL) skim milk whisked with 2 tsp. (10 mL) cornstarch or 1 tbsp. (15 mL) flour.
  OR use evaporated skim milk for creamy texture.
- **Cream Cheese**: Replace with low-fat yogurt cheese.
- **Creamy Soups**: Instead choose broth or tomato-based soups.
- **Dairy – Whole Milk, Cream and Full-Fat Cheese**: Fulfill your dairy needs with skim or 1% milk, low-fat yogurt or cottage cheese.
- **Fiber**: Instead of enriched white pasta, white rice, white bread and refined cereals, increase the fiber in your diet by substituting beans, lentils, peas, wheat bran, bran flake cereal, oat bran cereal, whole-wheat bread, raisins, oranges, grapefruits, pears, apples, raspberries, nectarines, salads with carrots, dried fruits, raw broccoli, cauliflower, chickpeas, tomatoes. For a healthier sandwich, place an assortment of chopped vegetables and/or fruits in a whole-wheat pita pocket. **Tip**: Keep vegetables crisp longer by putting a dry sponge in your crisper.
- **Flour**: Keep cakes from sticking to the pan by sprinkling wheat germ (in place of flour) on the pan after it is greased.
- **Fresh Fish**: If fresh fish is not readily available, use canned tuna, salmon or sardines. Be sure to choose fish canned in water instead of oil.
- **Fruit Juice (for cooking)**: To reduce sugar, replace 1 cup (250 mL) of juice with 1 cup (250 mL) spicy herb tea.
- **Garlic Toast**: To reduce calories, mist bread with vegetable cooking oil spray. Sprinkle with garlic powder and toast. **Tip**: If you add too much garlic to a recipe, sprinkle food with parsley.

- **MEAT**: Healthier alternatives include lower-fat skinless turkey, chicken, fish, beef (inside, outside round), rump roast, sirloin and pork tenderloin. **Tip**: To make any meat easier to dice or slice, place it in the freezer for about 1½ hours. Remove from the freezer and cut according to the recipe instructions.
- **MILK FOR BAKING**: 1 cup (250 mL) = 1 cup (250 mL) tea.
- **MSG**: Replace MSG for tenderizing meat. Marinate the meat in papaya juice. Strong tea can also be used as a tenderizing marinade.
- **OIL**: Non-stick vegetable cooking spray will reduce the fat in your recipe.
- **OIL**: For wok cooking, try vegetable broth, water, wine or fruit juice.
- **PARMESAN CHEESE**: Use Monterey Jack cheese instead to cut fat.
- **POPSICLES**: Forget about store-bought frozen treats loaded with sugar. Make healthy Popsicles by puréeing fresh or frozen fruit and freezing the purée or fruit juices in Popsicle holders.
- **SALT**: Replace half of the salt in your salt shaker with a salt substitute. **Tip**: If a dish tastes salty, add 2 tsp. (10 mL) of sugar. For salty soup, add a potato.
- **SALT**: Use lots of chopped celery leaves to replace salt in vegetable-based stews.
- **SUGAR**: Replace sugar or use less by adding vanilla or fruit to yogurt **OR** Add cinnamon or fruit to cereal. Sprinkle cinnamon on baked apples.
- **SWEETENER**: ½ cup (125 mL) sugar = ½ cup (125 mL) maple syrup **OR** ½ cup (125 mL) honey, ⅓ cup (75 mL) molasses (decrease or increase the amount of liquid or flour in a recipe according to the liquid content of the sweetener), ½ cup (125 mL) fruit juice concentrate or 1 cup (250 mL) sugarless fruit jam. **Tip**: When you substitute honey for sugar in a cookie recipe, your cookies will stay moist longer.
- **VEGETABLE OIL**: Use olive oil or canola oil – they have the best fat composition of "healthy" fats – monounsaturated and polyunsaturated fats, which actually help to control cholesterol levels.

Metric in the Kitchen

The most common measurement in metric recipes is the milliliter, or mL for short. Here is how it works: 1 tsp. = 5 mL; 1 tbsp. = 15 mL; 1 cup = 250 mL Large volumes of 1,000 mL or more are measured in liters, or L for short. Baking pans and casseroles are measured by volume, in liters.

VOLUME MEASUREMENTS:

1 fl. oz	= 28.41 mL	1 mL	= 0.04 fl. oz.
1 pt.	= 570 mL	1 L	= 1.75 pt.
1 qt.	= 1.14 L	1 L	= 0.88 qt.
1 Imp. Gal.	= 4.54 L	1 L	= 0.22 Imp. Gal.

Remember:

0.5 L or 500 mL, is smaller than 1 pint
0.1 L is smaller than 1 qt.
1.0 L is smaller than ¼ gal.

SPOONS:	Approximate Standard Conversion
¼ tsp.	1 mL (milliliters)
½ tsp.	2 mL
1 tsp.	5 mL
2 tsp.	10 mL
1 tbsp.	15 mL

CUPS:	Approximate Standard Conversion
¼ cup	50 mL (milliliters)
⅓ cup	75 mL
½ cup	125 mL
⅔ cup	150 mL
¾ cup	175 mL
1 cup	250 mL
4½ cups	1000 mL or 1 litre

The metric measurement for length that you will use most in the kitchen is the centimeter, or cm for short.

LENGTH MEASUREMENTS:

1 inch	= 2.54 cm	1 cm	= 0.39 in.
1 foot	= 0.30 metre	1 m	= 3.28 ft.
1 yard	= 0.91 m	1 m	= 1.09 yd.
1 mile	= 1.61 km	1 km	= 0.62 mi.

Pans, Casseroles:

8 x 8", 20 x 20 cm, 2 L
9 x 9", 22 x 22 cm, 2.5 L
9 x 13", 22 x 33 cm, 4 L
10 x 15", 25 x 38 cm, 1.2 L
11 x 17", 28 x 43 cm, 1.5 L
8 x 2" round, 20 x 5 cm, 2 L
9 x 2" round, 22 x 5 cm, 2.5 L
10 x 4½" tube, 25 x 11 cm, 5 L
8 x 4 x 3" loaf, 20 x 10 x 7 cm, 1.5 L
9 x 5 x 3" loaf, 23 x 12 x 7 cm, 2 L

Grams and kilograms (g and kg for short) are the metric measurements for weighing foods such meat, fish, poultry, cheese, butter, and cereals, etc.

Weight Measurements:

0.04 oz.	= 1 g
1 oz.	= 28.35 g
2 oz.	= 56.7 g
3 oz.	= 85 g
4 oz.	= 113.4 g
5 oz.	= 141.7 g
6 oz.	= 170.1 g
7 oz.	= 198.4 g
8 oz.	= 226.8 g
16 oz.	= 453.6 g
1 lb.	= 0.45 kg
32 oz.	= 917.2 g
1 kg	= 2.21 lb.

Remember:

100 g weighs a little less than ¼ lb.
250 g weighs a little more than ½ lb.
500 g weighs a little more than 1 lb.
1,000 g (1 kg) weighs a little more than 2 lbs.

Temperature in metric is measured in degrees Celsius. To convert Fahrenheit to Celsius, use the formula: Fahrenheit –32 X 5/9 = Celsius.

Some Temperature Equivalents:

175°F =	80°C
200°F =	100°C
225°F =	110°C
250°F =	120°C
275°F =	140°C
300°F =	150°C
325°F =	160°C
350°F =	180°C
375°F =	190°C
400°F =	200°C
425°F =	220°C
450°F =	230°C
475°F =	240°C
500°F =	260°C

Easy Substitution Recipes

CHEESE SAUCE

10 oz. (284 mL) condensed cream of mushroom, celery or chicken soup
½ cup (125 mL) grated medium Cheddar, Swiss or marble cheese
2 tbsp. (30 mL) cream or milk

Combine all ingredients in a saucepan over low heat. Stir often. Spoon over fish, vegetables, or use as a fondue with fresh vegetable dippers or as a chip dip. **Makes 1⅓ cups (325 mL).**

JAM

2 cups (500 mL) crushed berries (strawberries, raspberries, cranberries, gooseberries, blueberries)
3 cups (750 mL) white sugar

Crush fruit and boil for 1 minute. Heat sugar and add. Boil for 2 minutes. Remove from heat and beat for 4 minutes. Scoop into jars and seal.

Note: If you are using raspberries, add 2 tbsp. (30 mL) of vinegar before boiling to retain red color.

VEGGIE SOUP

1 quart (1 L) diced carrots
1 onion, chopped
1 quart (1 L) diced potatoes
1 quart (1 L) chopped string beans
1 quart (1 L) chopped celery
1 quart (1 L) fresh corn kernels
2 quarts (2 L) chopped, peeled tomatoes
2 red peppers, chopped
3 green pepper, chopped
1 tsp. (5 mL) pepper
2 tbsp. (30 mL) salt

Place veggies in a large pot, add cold water to cover. Bring to a boil, lower heat and simmer for 20 minutes. Pack in sealers and process in pressure canner following manufacturer's instructions for time and pressure. Adjust to altitude. **Tip:** You can substitute the beans for peas or replace some of the other vegetables for potatoes. Substitute any frozen ingredients for fresh.

Pizza Crust, No-Yeast

2¾ cup (675 mL) all-purpose flour
1¼ tsp. (6 mL) baking powder
¼ tsp. (1 mL) salt
⅔ cup (150 mL) warm water
2 tbsp. (30 mL) vegetable oil

Stir first 3 ingredients together. Make a well in the center of the bowl and add remaining ingredients. Mix until smooth and elastic. Add flour if the dough is sticky. Press over a greased pizza pan. Add toppings of your choice and bake at 350°F (180°C) for 15-20 minutes, or until browned.

The Number One Substitution Recipe – Great for Leftovers

Easy Quiche

8 eggs (or see page 121 for substitutions)
½ cup (125 mL) of any chopped, cooked meat (canned or fresh), e.g., ham, bacon, chicken
16 Ritz crackers or any other kind of cracker
1 cup (250 mL) shredded cheese (any kind)
½ cup (125 mL) diced green, red or white onions
salt and pepper to taste
½ cup (125 mL) half and half cream OR milk

Beat eggs and add all other ingredients. Pour into a 9" (23 cm) greased pie dish or 12-14 individual muffin cups. Bake at 350°F (180°C) for 20 minutes, or until the edges are brown. Remove from oven and let stand for 5 minutes.

Kitchen Substitutions

- **Bread Bag Closure**: If you lose a bread tag closure don't let your bread go stale, a barrette or twist tie will work well in its place.
- **Bowl Covers**: Use a clean shower cap as a bowl cover when refrigerating food.
- **Bowl Scraper**: Cut a plastic container lid in half. Leave the rim on the other side to use as a handle.
- **Cake Decorating Bag**: Cut off the corner of a plastic sandwich or milk bag. Use as is or insert a cake tip into the bag to decorate cakes and cookies.
- **Cake Pan**: Instead of a regular cake pan, use a metal bowl as a cake pan. Remove the cake from the bowl and decorate the top with big drops of light yellow icing. Your cake will look like a bowl of popcorn. The "bowl" cake can also form the skirt for a "Barbie" cake or put two bowl shapes together to create a basketball or pumpkin cake.
- **Cake Tester**: Use a raw spaghetti strand as you would use a toothpick. Insert the spaghetti into the cake; cake is done when it comes out clean.
- **Canisters**: Make yourself a set of same-sized canisters by saving 1-gallon milk jugs. Use them to store flour and other baking products. Milk jugs also work well for holding, laundry soap.
- **Coffee Filters**: You can still make great coffee if you run out of filters. Cut a paper towel to fit your coffee filter holder or insert a J-cloth.

  Tip: To avoid coffee being diluted by dropping ice cubes into super-hot coffee, freeze leftover coffee or tea into ice-cube trays.
- **Colander**: Save the plastic containers that strawberries come in and use them as small strainers.
- **Cookbook Protector**: Cover your cookbook with a transparent plastic bag before beginning your project. Use a mini photo album to organize recipe cards.
- **Cookie Cutter**: Create fun cookie cutters by using the cutters from play dough kits. Children's stacking cups and regular tumblers also work well.

- **Cookie Flattener:** A greased potato masher or fork is a smart substitute for your fingers or a floured glass when flattening cookies. The design will give your cookies an interesting pattern.
- **Cookie Shaper:** Bake perfectly shaped cookies by dropping dough into muffin pans instead of on a cookie sheet. Ice cream scoops of varying sizes also work well for dropping cookie dough onto pans.
- **Cookie Sheet:** Remove an oven rack from the oven and cover it with aluminum foil. Drop the cookies directly onto the large sheet.
- **Cooling Rack:** Remove an unused rack from the oven. Cover it with waxed paper and use it to cool cookies, cakes and muffins.
- **Cupcake Frosting:** Place a chocolate mint or marshmallow on each cupcake while still warm or place them in the hot oven for 1 minute.
- **Cutting Board:** Chop vegetables on the waxy side of freezer paper.
- **Drinking Glasses for Children:** Make a hole in the center of a small yogurt container lid. Fill the container with juice and close the lid. Insert a straw into the hole.
- **Fruit Cutter:** Instead of slicing a melon, use an ice cream scoop and create little balls. Fun for the kids to eat. **Tip**: Freeze pieces of watermelon to use as ice cubes in fruit drinks.
- **Funnel:** Cut the bottom off a plastic 2-quart (2 L) pop bottle and pour the ingredients through the wide end. When plastic bottles are not available, roll up a newspaper or sheet of paper to form a funnel.
- **Ice Tray:** Save Styrofoam egg cartons and reuse them as ice cube trays. They stack neatly and the attached lids will help avoid spillage.
- **Knife:** Use dental floss to cut cake layers in half for a multi-layered torte.
- **Knife Sharpener:** Run your knives along a leather belt when you need a sharpener.
- **Meatball Shaper:** For large round meatballs use an ice-cream scoop.
- **Meatloaf Pans:** Make tiny meatloaf appetizers or hamburger patties using a muffin tin.
  OR Use a tube pan, the meat will cook faster and be easy to cut.
- **Muffin Pans:** When you want to bake muffins but you do not have a muffin tin, use a regular baking sheet. Space jar sealers onto the sheet and place paper muffin cups in the sealers, then add batter.

- **Nonstick Cooking Spray:** Make your own using 1 cup (250 mL) vegetable oil and 1 cup (250 mL) liquid lecithin, pour into a spray bottle.
- **Pancake Cutter:** Let the kids cut their own pancakes with the help of a pizza cutter. Cookie cutters make fun pancake shapes.
- **Play Dough Recipe using Kool-Aid**

  ½ cup (125 mL) salt
  2 cups (500 mL) water
  Kool-Aid for color
  2 tbsp. (30 mL) vegetable oil
  2 cups (500 mL) flour
  2 tbsp. (30 mL) alum (available at grocery stores)

  Boil the salt in the water until dissolved. Add Kool-Aid color and all other ingredients. Knead until smooth. Store in a covered container in the refrigerator; lasts 2 months.
- **Potato Masher:** A pastry blender will mash potatoes, cooked carrots and eggs for egg salad.
- **Pudding Bars:** Clean and save Popsicle sticks and stick them into a freezer mold filled with pudding. Stand the Popsicle stick in the middle and freeze. Also use Popsicle sticks to make candied apples.
- **Rolling Pin:** Smooth out dough by filling a 2-quart (2 L) plastic bottle with water and placing it in a plastic bag. Be sure to sprinkle flour on the dough to avoid any sticking.
- **Salt and Pepper Shaker:** Make small holes in two film containers and fill them with salt and pepper.
- **Shelf Liners:** Save old tea towels and line your shelves with them instead of shelf paper. Every few months you can toss the cloth into the wash and freshen up your cupboards.
- **Sink Plug:** A wet tea bag placed in the drain will keep your sink from draining. A plastic disk cut from a yogurt lid will also work well.
- **Splatter Guard:** Turn a metal colander upside down over a frying pan to avoid grease splattering onto the stove.
- **Table Runner:** Cut a damaged or torn tablecloth in half. Hem the sides and display as a table runner.
- **Tea Cozy:** Keep tea warm by dressing the teapot in a winter toque.

Homemade Cleaning Substitutions

- **All-Purpose Cleaner:** Mix ⅓ cup (75 mL) baking soda, ⅔ cup (150 mL) borax, and ⅔ cup (150 mL) white vinegar. Store in a spray bottle.
- **Ceramic Tile Cleaner:** Apply isopropyl alcohol on a cotton ball or rag and rub over tiles.
- **Chrome Polish:** Use aluminum foil to buff chrome.
- **Copper or Brass Cleaner:** Sprinkle salt on a wet sponge and wipe.
- **Dish Detergent:** Mix 2 cups (500 mL) grated hard bar soap with 4 quarts (4 L) water. Heat until it boils. Lower heat and simmer for 10 minutes. Cool partially and pour into a bottle.
- **Dishwasher Rinse:** Into an empty dishwasher pour 1 cup (250 mL) of vinegar or 4 oz. (115 g) package of orange juice crystals. Run one full cycle.
- **Drain Cleaner:** Combine 1 tsp. (5 mL) baking soda with 1 cup (250 mL) vinegar and 4 quarts (4 L) hot water. Pour into drain.
- **Floor Wax:** Combine 1 part furniture polish to 2 parts vinegar. Spread evenly over the floor, as you would floor wax. Buff or polish as usual.
- **Furniture Polish:** Combine 1 cup (250 mL) of olive oil with 1 tsp. (5 mL) lemon-scented essential oil.
- **Glass Cleaner:** There are several alternatives to commercial window cleaners, including alcohol, ammonia and vinegar. Vinegar is often the choice of commercial window cleaners.
- **Gold Cleaner:** Stir together 1 tsp. (5 mL) baking soda with ½ cup (125 mL) water. Buff gold. **Note:** Always test cleaner on a small inconspicuous area before applying to entire surface.
- **Oven Cleaner:** Mix ¼ cup (60 mL) of baking soda with 1 cup (250 mL) of washing soda.

- **Room Deodorizer:** Simmer vinegar and water on the stove.
  OR Simmer cinnamon and cloves in water on the stove.
  OR Dissolve 1 tsp. (5 mL) baking soda and 1 tsp. (5 mL) lemon juice in a bowl. Slowly add 2 cups (500 mL) hot water. Pour into a spray bottle and spritz room.
  OR Put a few drops of your favorite essential oil on a light bulb. The heat from the light will activate the fragrance.
- **Starch:** Dissolve 1 cup (250 mL) of sugar in 2 quarts (2 L) of hot water. Pour the contents into a spray bottle.
- **Stickers:** To remove stickers from children's furniture, woodwork or even from car bumpers, use peanut butter or mayonnaise.
- **Toilet Bowl Cleaner:** Mix 1 cup (250 mL) of borax with ½ cup (125 mL) vinegar, pour into the bowl and brush.
  OR Pour vinegar or bleach into the tank and bowl to clean the toilet.
- **Window Cleaner:** Combine 1 quart (1 L) water, ½ cup (125 mL) ammonia and ⅓ cup (75 mL) vinegar.

All Around Substitutions

- **Air Freshener:** Save half the peel from an orange and fill it with salt, the citrus aroma lasts for months.
- **Aquarium Backdrop:** Save photos from old calendars and tape them to the outside back of the aquarium.
- **Birdfeeder:** Instead of having to refill a birdfeeder, make one that is inexpensive and completely edible. Tie a string around a bagel. Smear the bagel with peanut butter and sprinkle birdseed on it. Attach it to a tree branch.
- **Birthday Party Candleholders:** Insert birthday candles into colored mini marshmallows.
- **Bookends:** Decorate two large cans (with tight-fitting plastic lids) with wallpaper or fabric. Fill the cans with sand so that they are heavy enough to hold books.
- **Bookmark:** Keep track of your chapter by sliding a bobby pin onto the correct page.
- **Bookmarks:** Save Popsicle sticks and use them as bookmarks. You can write important chapter headings on the wood.
- **Boot Rack:** When you have lots of company, place outdoor footwear in the bathtub. They won't clutter up the entrance area and you can rinse the bathtub when the company leaves. You can also cut open large plastic lawn bags and place them on the floor in a bedroom to hold outdoor footwear.
- **Breath Freshener:** Chew parsley, peppermint, spearmint or fennel.
- **Broach:** A single earring will work nicely as a broach or scarf closure.
- **Bucket:** Never throw away gallon ice-cream buckets, they are handy for carrying cleaning supplies around the house, packing meals for transporting and filling with soap and water for household chores.
- **Candleholders:** Take a pair of candles and wrap the lower half of each candle with aluminum foil. Place each in a wine glass and place enough aluminum foil in the bottom of the wine glasses to hold the candles in place. **Tip**: Put petroleum jelly around the lip of a candleholder to keep wax from sticking to it.

- **Car Door Opener:** If your keys are locked in and you own an older car, use the dipstick from the engine oil to pry the lock open.
- **Catnip:** Grow a catmint plant in your garden. Dry and crush the leaves. Put the leaves into a piece of felt and sew up the sides.
- **Closet Rod:** Set a broom handle on the brackets inside a closet – this can also work as a curtain rod.
- **Clothes Hanger:** Create extra storage in your garage by hanging an extension ladder from the ceiling. Use it as hanging space for drying clothes or as a place to hang ropes and tarps.
- **Clothes Storage Boxes:** Use the space under your bed to store out-of-season clothing. Suitcases make great storage boxes.
- **Compact Disk Holder:** A large plastic recipe holder makes an ideal CD organizer.
- **Cookbook Holder:** Using a fold-over pant hanger, place an open cookbook inside the clamp and close. Hang the hanger from a cupboard handle at eye level so that you can read the book without it getting splattered.
- **Cord Holder:** Coil an electrical cord and store it inside an empty toilet paper roll.
- **Dog Collar:** Depending on the type of suitcase you have, you may be able to remove the handle and put it to use as an emergency collar, leash or both for your pet.
- **Dog Dish:** For an outdoor dog dish, place a wooden stake in the center of a tube pan. The dog will not be able to knock it over.
- **Dog Leash:** Store plastic bags in your car. If you unexpectedly need a dog leash, tie several plastic bags together to create a line. Plastic bags also come in handy when you need to clean up a doggy mess.
- **Dog Scoop:** Turn an empty bleach or fabric softener container upside down. Cut the jug in half.
- **Drawer Knobs:** Big wooden beads can easily be attached to a child's dresser drawers to add color to the room.
- **Dryer Cleaner:** Clean out dryer lint by using a dog's grooming brush.

- **Dryer Sheets:** Put old dryer sheets into a plastic bag with a bit of liquid fabric softener. Let them soak. Remove the sheets from the bag and lay them flat to dry. Reuse. You can also save money by tearing dryer sheets in half instead of using a whole sheet.
- **Earring Organizer:** Never sift through a mess again. Sort your earrings into a nuts and bolts drawer organizer.
- **Eraser:** Rub out mistakes with a rubber band, rubber ball or, if you are really desperate, the side of your sneaker.
- **Eyeglass Case:** Keep eyeglasses and eyeglass cleaning solution in a small cotton swab box. Line the box with a soft cleaning cloth. Store the box in a desk or glove compartment.
- **Fan Belt:** an emergency fan belt can be made from pantyhose – twist the pantyhose and tie it as tightly as possible around the fan pulleys. Trim off the excess.
- **Firewood Carrier:** Use an old laundry basket to carry firewood from the basement or garage. The holder has firm handles and is easy to clean.
- **Fish Bowl:** You can create a unique centerpiece for your coffee table by placing colored stones in the bottom of a glass vase, trifle dish or glass fruit bowl; add water and fish. If you need a larger home for several fish, use an infant's bathtub.
- **Fish Food:** Poke small holes into a film container and fill it with fish food. The dispenser will make feeding easy for the kids.
- **Floral Styrofoam:** For an economical substitute, put plastic wrap at the bottom of a vase to help the flowers stand. Glass marbles also work well and they are reusable.
- **Foot Massager:** Place a rolling pin under your desk. This reflexology tip triggers the release of endorphins and reduces stress.
- **Gift Wrap:** When you need to wrap an unexpected present in a hurry, use aluminum foil. Add metallic ribbon.
- **Glue:** Save the water from cooked white rice and give it to your children for their craft projects.
- **Glue:** Blend 3 tbsp. (45 mL) cornstarch with 4 tbsp. (60 mL) cold water. Add 2 cups (500 mL) of boiling water.

- **Golf Ball Holder:** Whether you are a golf ball collector or just have a few, store them in egg cartons, they stack well.
- **Greeting Cards:** Compare the cost of greeting cards with that of postcards, you can find humorous and attractive illustrations. Photographs also double as greeting cards. Mount them on heavy paper. The receiver will appreciate the added thoughtfulness.
- **Hooks:** When you run out of hooks or pegs for your pegboard, use golf tees.
- **Hot Water Bottle:** Fill a 2-quart (2 L) pop bottle with hot water. Close the lid tightly. Wrap a hot-water bottle in a towel or a diaper to protect your skin.
- **Ice Pack:** Instead of holding ice cubes wrapped in a washcloth on a bruise, try a more flexible solution – hold a bag of frozen vegetables on the sore area.
- **Key Chain:** A firm bracelet with a strong open and close clasp works well and looks more attractive than a regular key chain. Place it on your wrist when you don't have pockets.
- **Kindling:** Recycle orange and lemon peels by using them as kindling in your fire. Cardboard egg cartons are another option.
- **Kitty Litter:** Shred newspaper and mix it with baking soda.
- **Level:** Fill a 2-quart (2 L) bottle ¾ full. Lay it on its side to determine when your project is level.
- **Litter Pan Liners:** Keep ahead of your cat by lining litter pans with garbage bags. Cleanup will be a snap.
- **Markers:** Dried-up markers can be dipped in white vinegar for 10 seconds to revive.
- **Masking Tape:** Cut wallpaper into thin strips, wet and apply where you need tape.
- **Matches:** Give yourself time to light a fire or several candles by lighting a piece of raw spaghetti.
- **Napkins:** Purchase plain paper napkins and personalize them by using a rubber stamp and stamp pad.
- **Necklace String:** For strong string use dental floss.
- **Office Organizer:** Clean out your desk and organize thumbtacks, staples, paper clips, etc. into muffin tin cups.

- **Packing Material:** Instead of newspaper or foam chips use popcorn or peanuts.
- **Paint Container:** Secure the lid on a bleach or fabric softener jug. Cut the jug in half horizontally and turn it upside down. Pour a small amount of paint into the container, it makes a light easy-to-carry tool for small jobs. For really small paint jobs pour a little of your paint into a nail polish bottle.
- **Paint Tray:** When you are ready to paint, but lack a proper paint tray, don't give up – use a baking pan or breakfast tray covered with a garbage bag.
- **Pencil Sharpener:** Slide a potato peeler or knife downward to sharpen pencils, crayons and pencil crayons.
- **Pincushion:** Use a bar of soap as a pincushion, it is inexpensive and the soap helps the needles to slide in and out of fabric easily. A cork or eraser will also hold pins.
- **Place Cards:** Locate a photograph of each of the guests coming to your party. Fold a piece of heavy paper in half and tape the photo onto it.
- **Popsicle Drip Holder:** Cut a slit in a plastic lid or a coffee filter for the Popsicle stick to go through.
- **Puppy Bed:** Use a baby's bathtub as a birthing bed for puppies.
- **Rags:** Save old T-shirts, towels and socks.
- **Raincoat:** Cut a neck and armholes into a garbage bag and store it inside your purse to protect your clothing against sudden rain showers.
- **Rash Ointment:** Next time someone in your family gets the chicken pox or an itchy rash, put 1 cup (250 mL) of oatmeal into a sock. Tie the sock closed and float it in the bathtub. The oatmeal will soothe the rash without clogging the drain.

- **Ribbon**: After you wrap a gift, cut strips of wrapping paper and curl them with the edge of the scissors to make a matching bow or ribbon.
- **Saw Cover**: Cut a piece of garden hose and slit it lengthwise to fit over the blade of a saw or an axe.
- **Saw Horse**: Place a ladder on its side and lay your wood on top.
- **Screwdriver**: Use a butter knife in place of a screwdriver.
- **Security Box**: Tear the pages out of the center of a large book and store important papers inside.
- **Sewing Kit**: For travelling put together a collection of buttons, needles and thread. Store inside a film container.
- **Sick Room Table**: Use an ironing board covered with plastic as a table for someone who is in bed sick. Adjust the table to the proper height and cover it with plastic or with towels.
- **Silver Cleaner**: This works like magic on blackened silver. Do not use too frequently. Place slightly crumpled aluminum foil in a plastic bucket. Dissolve ¼ cup (60 mL) washing soda in 4 quarts (1 L) of hot water. Place silver on foil and let stand for a few seconds, until tarnish is gone. Remove silver, rinse and dry. To deter tarnish and for best results, you can polish quickly with silver polish. Replace foil as it loses its shine. Use rubber gloves to protect your hands.
- **Shoe Buffer**: An oven mitten or washcloth mitten can double as a shoe polisher. Spread one side with polish and buff with the other side.
- **Shoehorn**: A metal spoon will make sliding on shoes easier. You can also create a shoehorn by cutting the rim off a plastic container lid.
- **Shovel**: If you find yourself stuck in dirt or snow, use one of your hubcaps to dig your way out.
- **Socks:** To keep socks from being mismatched or lost, pin them together before laundering them.
- **Squeaky Car Door:** When you do not have oil on hand, use the dipstick from your engine oil to lubricate the hinges.

- **Squirt Gun**: Any well-rinsed cleaning bottle should be saved as a squirt bottle for doing your hair, watering plants, making your own cleaning products or squirting spot cleaner onto your clothes. To clear spray nozzles, dip in rubbing alcohol; let sit 5 minutes and rinse under hot water.
- **String Dispenser**: Place a ball of yarn or string inside a piggy bank. Through the slot, draw the string out as needed.
- **Table**: If you have a large gathering and need a larger table, lay an old door (minus the door knobs, of course) on top of your existing table.
- **Tablecloth**: Iron a beautiful bed sheet to cover a large table.
- **Tape Measure**: When you are trying to measure an area by yourself, use string. Tape one end to the starting point and carry the string as far as you want to measure. String also works well for measuring curves.
- **Terrarium**: A fish aquarium may become the focal point of a room by filling it with decorative plants, shells, colored gravel or stones. An aquarium also doubles well as a container for a herb garden.
- **Thimble**: Cut the thumb off a rubber glove.
- **Thread**: Dental floss is a strong substitute for regular-weight sewing thread. Fishing line is a strong and transparent option to regular sewing thread.
- **Toothbrush**: Don't discard old toothbrushes, they have many uses – apply shoe polish, clean a cheese grater, clean jewellery. it is just the right size for scrubbing around bathroom fixtures and grout. The flexible bristles make it a good nail brush and perfect for rubbing detergent into laundry stains.
- **Toothpaste**: If your toothpaste tube is empty, place the tube in a glass of hot water (opening down). The heat will release the paste stuck along the sides and you can brush one more time.
- **Toothpicks**: Pieces of raw spaghetti will clean your teeth, hold up plastic on cakes and act as cake testers.

- **Travel Bag:** Sew two pieces of fabric together and insert a sealable freezer bag. The pouch is inexpensive, waterproof and has a built-in closure for toiletries.
- **Tray:** Serve food to guests and family by putting a beautiful old mirror or picture frame to a new use.
- **Twist Tie:** A pipe cleaner works just as well.
- **Umbrella Stand:** Put rocks inside a large boot. Place your umbrellas inside.
- **Vase:** A trifle dessert dish can double as a vase. Flowers may be arranged well above the rim or in line with the rim. A new trend is to submerge large leaves sideways under water, along the edge of the glass.
- **Wall Hangings:** Be creative and make a statement about yourself with the artwork that you choose. Frame postcards, mirrors, beautiful wallpaper, handmade paper, posters, dried flowers or leaves or enlarged black and white or color photographs.
- **Wallpaper:** Apply wallpaper paste to the separated pages of a colorful children's book, a calendar or a hobby magazine, e.g., flowers or horses. Mount the pages on the wall. This is a very inexpensive way to decorate a nursery.

- **Wallpaper Border:** Measure and cut strips of wallpaper into border widths. The project will be more affordable.
- **Wood Filler:** Combine sawdust and glue. Add coffee or tea to tint the filler to the proper color.

Cosmetic Substitutions

- **Blush:** Mix lipstick with cold cream and apply it to your cheeks.
- **Body Paint:** Combine Crisco with food coloring. Heat the Crisco in the microwave, pour into an empty film container and mix with food color.
- **Cold Cream:** Use a small amount of vegetable shortening.
- **Cream Rinse:** Combine laundry fabric softener with water in a bottle.
- **Dandruff Controller:** Apply dried rosemary to scalp and rinse.
  Tip: Rosemary also works well to enhance hair color.
  OR apply 1 cup (250 mL) vinegar; leave 15 minutes and rinse.
- **Deodorant:** You do not need to call in sick when you run out of deodorant. Baking soda will work in its place.
- **Eyebrow Brush:** Save your money use an old toothbrush on eyebrows.
- **Eyebrow Pencil:** Use a soft lead pencil for your eyebrows or eyeliner.
- **Eye Pads:** Place cooled green tea bags or cucumber slices on tired eyes to help reduce swelling and puffiness.
- **Hair Conditioner:** Soften your hair by applying mayonnaise or a whole egg. Rinse well.
- **Hair Gel:** Dissolve ¼-½ tsp. (1-2 mL) of unflavored gelatin in 1 cup (250 mL) of warm water. Keep refrigerated.
- **Hair Growth Enhancer:** Scrub fresh catnip on your scalp; rinse; repeat.
- **Hair Lightener:** Combine lemon juice and vegetable oil. Apply to hair. Leave on for 20 minutes. Shampoo and rinse.
- **Nail File:** Use the side of a matchbox as an emergency emery board.
- **Rosier Complexion:** Add 1 tsp. (5 mL) granulated sugar to a regular cleanser and blend in your hands. Lather up and wash as usual.

- **Shaving Nicks**: Apply a wax-based lip balm to nicks.
- **Shiny Hair**: Mash an avocado in a bowl, add 1 tbsp. (15 mL) olive oil and 1 tsp. (5 mL) baking powder. Mix well, work into hair. Put on a shower cap for 10 minutes. Rinse (no need to shampoo).
- **Smelly Feet**: Soak feet in 3 oz. (85 g) package of jelly powder dissolved in 2 cups (500 mL) water.

- **Smooth Skin**: Beat egg whites and apply to face. Leave on for 5 minutes; rinse. Your pores will have a tighter appearance.
- **Tonic for Hair**: Scrub dried yarrow on scalp and rinse.

Bathroom Substitutions

- **Bath Oil:** For a **Tropical Oil**, combine 2 tbsp. (30 mL) EACH canola and apricot oils. Add 10 drops EACH mango, gardenia and coconut oils. Bottle until ready to use. Shake before pouring into running bath water.
- **Bath Pillow:** Soak comfortably on a partially inflated beach ball.
- **Bathroom Air Freshener:** Keep a box of matches and a scented candle in the bathroom and light as needed. (Keep matches out of reach of children.)
- **Bathroom Organizer:** A three-tiered hanging egg basket works well in the bathroom to organize shampoo and soap (also a good way to keep razors out of reach of small children).
- **Bubble Bath – Floral:** Combine 1 quart (1 L) distilled water, 1 cup (250 mL) unscented shampoo, 6 tbsp. (90 mL) liquid glycerin, 5 drops floral oil of your choice (rose, lavender, lilac, orange, lemon, almond, etc.). Bottle until ready to use. Shake before pouring into running bath water.

- **Bubble Bath – Foaming Honey Vanilla:** Combine 1 cup (250 mL) canola oil, ½ cup (125 mL) EACH honey and liquid soap, 1 tbsp. (15 mL) vanilla extract. Bottle until ready to use. Shake before pouring ¼ cup (60 mL) into running bathwater.
- **Soap Dish:** A big shell makes a fancy soap dish.
- **Soap Holder:** A sponge makes a smart soap holder – you do not have to scrape soap off of the soap dish and when the sponge is full of soap you can just toss it into the washing machine.
- **Toothbrush Holder:** Cut a slit in the lid of an empty pill holder or film container. Slide the toothbrush through the slit; close the container over it.
- **Toothpaste:** Baking soda works well in place of toothpaste. In fact, some toothpastes advertise that they contain baking soda.

Family Survival Substitutions

- **Baby Bed**: Instead of toting a crib with you while travelling, bring a playpen or pull out a dresser drawer for your baby to sleep in.
- **Baby Crawler Knee Pads**: The wristbands that athletes use work wonderfully well to protect baby's knees.
- **Baby Playpen**: When baby is learning to sit up, use a small empty bathtub for support.
- **Baby Powder**: Use cornstarch instead of baby powder when changing a diaper.
- **Baby Powder Dispenser**: Poke small holes into a plastic film container. Siblings will be able to help diaper the baby.
- **Baby Wipes**: Heat cold baby wipes in the microwave for a few seconds.
- **Bib**: An apron doubles as a large bib for small children or elders.
- **Birthday Party Tablecloth**: Here is an affordable way to keep young guests entertained while you serve food – cover the table with white paper. Distribute crayons, stickers and markers along the table.
- **Child's Table and Chairs**: The wooden spools that hold cable or rope for commercial use can be painted and made into furniture.
- **Cold Blankets**: Heat blankets in the dryer for children or babies. This works especially well for newborns or people who are sick. (Be sure the blankets are not too hot.)
- **Diaper Rash**: As a preventative, use petroleum jelly, it's effective and inexpensive.
- **First Aid**: Use a red washcloth to wipe a bleeding cut on a child.
- **Fun Meal**: Instead of taking your children out for lunch, make a special meal for them at home. Join them in making and organizing an indoor or outdoor tea party or picnic.

- **Kids Crafts:** Save Popsicle sticks for making puppets and create wooden structures by gluing Popsicle sticks together.
- **Knives:** Give your child a Popsicle stick or tongue depressor to use to apply butter, honey or peanut butter on bread.
- **Lego:** Collect small scrap pieces of wood. Sand the edges to avoid splinters. Give the collection to your kids for building blocks. For an additional activity, the kids can paint the blocks.
- **Maze:** Collect as many boxes as you can and create a maze for children to go through. Put a small prize at the end.
- **Night Light:** Use a dimmer switch to control the amount of light in a room.
- **Organizer:** Hang a plastic shoe holder over the bedroom or bathroom door to hold washcloths, lotion, wipes, diapers, toys, etc. This also works in the car to hold toys, books and snacks.
- **Paint Holder:** Keep paint separated by filling muffin cups with a variety of colors. For bathtub fun pour shaving cream into each muffin cup. Use food coloring to make different colors and let your child paint the bathtub walls. (Always supervise small children in the bathtub).
- **Paper Dolls:** With your pre-school child, spend time cutting pictures of people out of magazines. Children love imagination games.
- **Playhouse:** Help your child build a fort using blankets, tables, chairs, sheets and tablecloths.
- **Play Tents:** Cover furniture with a picnic tablecloth, curtains or sheets.
- **Safety Latches on Cupboards:** Use elastic bands or string to keep cupboard doors safely closed.
- **Soup Spoon:** It takes a lot of balance for a child to eat soup with a spoon. Serve soup in a mug with a straw.

- **Swimming Pool:** When the weather is too cold to go outside, bring the fun inside. Get a baby's plastic bathtub and fill it half full of water. Add food coloring. Offer your child an eyedropper, turkey baster, colander, measuring spoons, funnels and cups. For a smaller water play center, fill a bowl with water and cornstarch. The water will feel like slime running through their fingers.
- **Teething Ring:** Offer a baby a frozen bagel, frozen waffle, frozen banana, frozen washcloth or a stripped corncob to soothe aching gums.
- **Towels:** Use safety pins to pin a towel onto a child's towel rack so that the towel won't fall down.
- **Tub Toys:** Use a mesh laundry bag to hold tub toys. Hang it on the shower and the toys will drain and be out of the way.

Garden Substitutions and Hints

- **Cats**: Here are several suggestions for keeping cats out of your garden: Spray plants with a solution of cayenne pepper and water – non-toxic and effective. Reapply after waterings or rain.
  OR combine 2 parts cayenne pepper, 3 parts dry mustard, 5 parts flour. Sprinkle where needed and reapply after waterings or rain.
  OR place mothballs around the edges of the garden.
  OR place pine cones on the top of the soil for potted plants to keep cats out of the pots.
  OR place pine cones or coarse mulch under bushes and shrubs to keep cats away.
- **Compost**: Substitute good for garbage by composting the following: grass clippings, egg shells, sawdust, plant trimmings, coffee grounds/filters, fruit and vegetable scraps, leaves, tea leaves/bags, hay, straw, floor sweepings, vacuum cleaner contents, pet and human hair.
- **Compost Bin**: Create a bin to suit the size that you need using concrete blocks or recycled wooden vertical pallets.
- **Flavor Enhancer**: Add wood ashes to fruit trees in the garden.

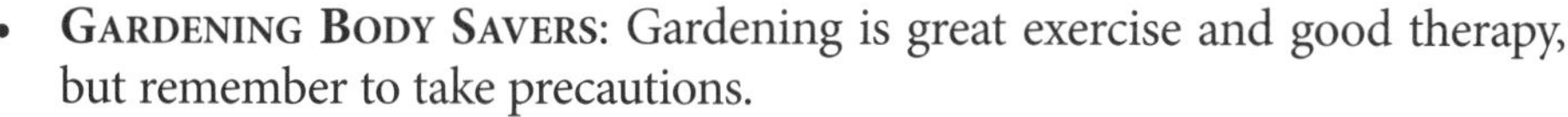

- **Gardening Body Savers**: Gardening is great exercise and good therapy, but remember to take precautions.
  - Do warm-up exercises, stretch, apply sunscreen and vary your activities to avoid repetitive muscle strain.
  - Use your legs, not your back, when lifting.
  - Long-handled weeding tools are helpful. Use a potting table that is at a comfortable height.
  - Wear gardening gloves and a hat for protection.
  - Drink water before, during and after working outside.
- **Garden Kneepads**: Wrap an old pillow in a plastic bag and place the pillow under your knees while you are gardening.

- **Garden Stakes:** As the children finish eating Popsicles, save the sticks and mark your garden with them in the spring.
- **Mosquito Repellent:** Make your own – in a spray bottle combine.
  4 qts. (4 L) water,
  4 tbsp. (60 mL) lemon dish soap,
  2 tbsp. (30 mL) original Listerine,
  Spray liberally (safe for small children).
- **Mosquito Repellents:** For the yard, instead of spraying poisons, burn citronella candles to repel the little critters. Put birdseed in the garden. Build a purple martin house in your yard. Also read the Plant Partners hint on the next page.
  AND, for humans, avoid wearing perfume. Wear light-colored clothing, eat an orange (mosquitoes do not like the smell of citrus). Rub lemon soap on any exposed skin.
- **Mulch in Gardens:** You do not need to use commercial products to be satisfied with your mulch. Use flat stones, boards, leaves, grass clippings, straw, hay, wood shavings or chips, seaweed, burlap, old pieces of carpet or black and white newspaper (colored inks may contain toxic compounds).
- **Pesticide Substitute:**
  Mites: Mix ½ cup (125 mL) buttermilk and 4 cups (1 L) wheat flour with 5 gallons water.
  Beetles: Boil ¼ lb. (125 g) cedar chips in 1 gallon (15 L) water for 3 hours. Strain. Dilute with 2 parts water. Pour into spray bottle.
  Sucking and Chewing Insects: In 1 gallon (15 L) of water, put 1 garlic clove and crushed hot peppers. Pour into spray bottle.
  Aphids and Spiders: Mix ¼ lb. (125 g) glue in 1 gallon of water. Sprinkle onto the area.
- **Weed Zapper:** For a very effective, easy-to-make **Weed Killer**, combine.
  4 cups (1 L) white vinegar,
  ¼ cup (60 mL) salt and
  2 tbsp. (30 mL) dishwashing liquid in a spray bottle.
  Spray on **unwanted** plants in a patio or in driveway cracks, etc. Be careful to NOT spray on adjacent plants.

- **Plant Partners:** Some plants complement one another. Companion planting provides natural growth, flavor and protection benefits, e.g., herbs, except fennel, planted at the corners of flower or vegetable gardens, help attract bees and discourage other insects. Here are a few examples:

  Herbs:

  Basil – plant with tomatoes, improves flavor and growth, repels mosquitoes and flies.

  Chives – plant with carrots, improves flavor and growth.

  Dill – plant with cabbage, improves growth. Don't plant near carrots.

  Garlic – plant near roses, repels aphids.

  Mint – plant near tomatoes and cabbages for healthy plants, repels cabbage moths.

  Vegetables:

  Asparagus – plant with tomatoes, basil, parsley; NOT with potatoes.

  Carrots – plant with lettuce, peas, onions, tomatoes; NOT with radishes, dill, parsnip, sage, rosemary, chives.

  Lettuce – plant with strawberries, onion, carrots, cabbage NOT with parsley, beets, beans, parsnips.

  Peas – plant with corn, carrots, beans, radish, cucumber; NOT with onions, garlic, shallots.

  Tomato – plant with asparagus, basil, cabbage; NOT with beets, broccoli, cauliflower, potato, carrots, chives, dill, rosemary, onions, parsley, nasturtiums.

  Attracting Insects:

  Bees – borage, catnip, dill, sage, hyssop, sweet william.

  Butterflies – basil, salvia, hyssop, sweet william.

  Lady Bugs – artemisia, yarrow, golden rod, morning glory.

  Repelling Insects:

  Ants – catnip, mint, onion, borage.

  Aphids – anise, catnip, mint, marigold, garlic, nasturtium, petunia, onion, oregano.

  Mosquitoes – basil, garlic, lemon thyme, geranium, catnip, marigold, penny royal, tansy.

- **Plant Pots:** The way that plants are displayed can make a great conversation piece. Contain your green friends in broken teacups, old teapots or kettles. Look around the yard for a worn out ankle boot, a rusty wheelbarrow, garden carts, tires and barrels.

- **Rabbit Repellent:** Sprinkle ground pepper around plants. OR Fill glass bottles half-full with water, set them in the ground throughout the garden. The whistle from the wind will scare away the rabbits.
- **Seedling Starter:** Put old muffin tins to good use by planting seeds in them. Egg cartons also work well, and if you plant the seeds in an emptied eggshell you can place them directly into the ground.
  OR Plant seeds in a milk carton cut in half. **OR** Place seeds into small or large yogurt containers.
  OR Clean and cut a plastic milk, bleach or fabric softener jug in half.
  OR Use a foil pan with peat pellets.
- **Seed Spreader:** The kids will be able to help out with gardening if you fill an empty film container with small holes and fill it with seeds.
- **Strawberries:** Place rubber snakes throughout your strawberry patch to keep the birds from pecking fruits. **OR** paint small stones red and place them among the plants before the berries ripen. Birds will pick at the stones and become discouraged before berries are ready to eat.

- **Tea Time (and Coffee):** Water indoor plants and outdoor pots with cooled leftover tea. Tea leaves and coffee grounds are acidic, use them around acid-loving plants, e.g., roses, berries, potatoes, rhododendrons, azaleas. Coffee grounds are rich in nitrogen, so they give a head start to compost. Don't use them directly on potted plants as they have a high salt level.

Outdoor Substitutions

- CAMPING MATCHES: You can make a fire even when you do not have matches. Find and gather up tinder (cattail, thistle, milkweed, dead grass clippings). Fluff the tinder into a pile. Strike a sharp rock against the hard edge of a knife. Aim toward the tinder. When you see a puff of smoke, blow short breaths until a flame ignites.
- CHILDREN'S GAMES: When you have no television or computer the children may become bored. Most of the following games require fewer than two pieces of equipment: Cat's Cradle, Hide and Go Seek, Tag, relay race, obstacle course, treasure hunt, nature collecting, scavenger hunt, throwing rocks into a hole, bubble blowing using a dish detergent solution (use a straw or wire to form a circle), butterfly catching, bug collecting, creating a Cheerio necklace.
- CLOTHESLINE: Attach a piece of string from one branch to another. Place shower hooks on the line for hanging clothing.
- COMMUNICATION DEVICE: Carry a mirror in your pocket when you go camping. It is small, light and will come in handy if you need to signal someone by using the reflection of sunlight.
- COMPASS: Push a stick into the ground. Mark the place where the shadow falls. Wait one hour and again mark the place where the shadow falls. The line between the marks is east/west. The stick is on the south side of the line.
- COOKING OIL: Obtain cooking oil in the wilderness by using a rock to smash walnuts, butternuts or hickory nuts.
- DISHWASHING SOAP: Add campfire ashes or sand to water.
- DOORMAT: To keep dirt and muck out of your tent or camper, lay a sturdy bathmat outside the entrance. It is easy to shake clean and launder.
- FIRE EXTINGUISHER: Throw baking soda onto a fire to put it out.
- FLASHLIGHT: Apply a piece of glow-in-the-dark tape around a flashlight so that you can find it in the dark.
- FOOT HEATER: On cold nights, find a medium-sized rock and heat it on the campfire. Remove the rock from the fire and carefully wrap it in a towel. Slide the covered rock into the bottom of your sleeping bag. Your feet should stay warm all night.

- **Gloves**: Cover your hands with plastic bags when doing dishes.
- **Ice**: Frozen juice makes an efficient ice pack for a day outside. When you are ready to eat make yourself a pitcher of nice cool juice.
- **Insect Bite Medicine**: Remove the stinger if present. DON'T squeeze it. Wash the bite area with soap and water, then rinse with cool water to reduce swelling. Apply ice if swelling is severe. Dab a bit of vinegar onto the bite to take away the itch.
  OR put a drop of lavender essential oil on the area to stop itching and reduce swelling.
  OR put a dab of toothpaste on the sting.
  OR use a paste of baking soda and water.
- **Insect Repellent**: Leave open cans or bottles of beer around where you are sitting. The smell of alcohol will attract stinging insects and they will drown in the liquid.
- **Lettuce**: For a healthy survival salad eat dandelions, chickweed or clover. Only consume outdoor vegetation where no chemicals have been sprayed.
- **Meat**: When there is no food, remember that all **healthy** birds, insects and mammals are edible.
- **Overnight Fire**: Dig a narrow trench. Put kindling and wood in the trench on sand or gravel. Clear a circle and light a fire. When cooking, place large smooth rocks on top of the pit to act as a grill.
- **Overnight Fridge**: Seal food in a waterproof bag, using a rock for weight. Immerse the bag in the lake.
- **Pan Cleaner**: To remove the black soot from pots easily, smear the bottoms of cooking pots with a bar of soap before putting them on the fire.
- **Pillow**: Stuff an old T-shirt with the fluffy white seed heads of cattails to make a pillow.
- **Pot Scrubber**: When in need, use a handful of broken eggshells or sand in place of steel wool.
- **Shower**: A bucket or garbage bag filled with water and hanging from a tree branch makes an instant shower.

- **Sling:** Use a leather belt to hold an injured arm in place.
- **Splint:** When you do not have access to a hospital and you require a splint, wrap the injured arm or leg in blankets or newspaper. Find smooth wood from trees to keep the bone in place. Use torn fabric strips to secure the splint.
- **Survival Snack:** Try acorns when you need a snack. Crack the shells lengthwise then squeeze the tips to extract the meat.
- **Tea and Coffee:** Use the leaves of all members of the mint family. Pour boiling water over them and let soak for 5 to 10 minutes. Also try raspberry leaves.
- **Toilet:** Dig a hole in the ground. Use leaves as toilet paper. Before leaving, carefully burn the leaves or toilet paper and fill the hole.
- **Water:** In a survival situation there is no substitute for water. Lay a cloth on the grass overnight. By morning the cloth should have soaked up enough dew for you to have a drink.
  OR Dig a hole and stand a plastic container or bottle in the center. Spread a piece of plastic, large enough to cover the hole, over the bottle. Put a hole in the plastic just at the mouth of the bottle. Secure with string or an elastic band. Secure the plastic with heavy rocks. By morning the accumulated condensation should have drained water into the bottle
- **Water Hauler:** Fill an empty 4-quart (4 L) milk jug with water and freeze it before going on a trip. Put the jug into your cooler as an ice pack. Drink the ice-cold water from the jug when you reach your destination. Once empty, use the jug to haul water. Dispose of it before heading home.
- **Waterproof Matches:** Dip ordinary matches in shellac and let them dry.

Index

CENTAX BOOKS MAKE GREAT GIFTS

Household Solutions & Substitutions	x $14.95 =	$
Grandma's Best	x $21.95 =	$
Grandma's Kitchen	x $21.95 =	$
Grandma's Soups & Stews with Salads, Breads & Biscuits	x $21.95 =	$
Grandma's Touch	x $21.95 =	$
201 Fat-Burning Recipes	x $19.95 =	$
201 MORE Fat-Burning Recipes	x $19.95 =	$
Create Your Own – College Survival Recipes	x $12.95 =	$
Create Your Own – Holiday Cookbook	x $12.95 =	$
Create Your Own – Recipes By Me Cookbook	x $12.95 =	$
Shipping and handling charge (total order)	=	$
Subtotal	=	$ $4.00
In Canada add 7% GST	=	$
Total enclosed	=	$

U.S. and international orders payable in U.S. funds/Prices subject to change.

NAME: __________
STREET: __________
CITY: __________ PROV./STATE __________
COUNTRY: __________ POSTAL CODE/ZIP: __________

❐ CHEQUE *OR* Charge to ❐ VISA ❐ MASTERCARD

Account Number: | | | | | | | | | | | | | | | | |

Expiry Date: | | | | |

Telephone (in case we have a question about your order): __________

Make cheque or money order payable

TO: **Centax Books & Distribution**
1150 Eighth Avenue
Regina, Saskatchewan
Canada S4R 1C9

OR Order by phone, fax or email:
Phone: 1-800-667-5595
FAX: 1-800-823-6829
E-mail: centax@printwest.com

See our website for our complete range of cookbooks,
gardening books, history books, etc.

www.centaxbooks.com

For fund-raising or volume purchases, contact Centax Books & Distribution for volume rates.
Please allow 2-3 weeks for delivery.

CENTAX COOKBOOKS MAKE GREAT GIFTS

201 Fat-burning Recipes

by Cathi Graham

Master your metabolism. Cathi Graham lost 186 pounds and has kept it off for over 10 years without dieting. This book complements her Fresh Start™ program. Although there were no foods she wouldn't allow herself, she ate a high-calorie intake of proven "fat-burning" foods. These easy recipes feature fibre-rich or high carbohydrate/low-fat foods. Calorie and fat counts are included. Here are great recipes for losing weight or just for maintaining a healthy lifestyle.

Retail $19.95 5¾" x 8½"
248 pages 5 colour photographs
ISBN 1-895292-34-4 perfect bound

Grandma's Kitchen – Comfort Cooking from Canadian Grandmas – over 200,000 sold in series

by Irene Hrechuk and Verna Zasada

Grandma's Kitchen celebrates Canadian cooking as traditional favorites from many other countries become new Canadian traditions. *Grandma's kitchen* evokes memories of delicious flavors and aromas. With this cookbook you can prepare your special childhood favorites as grandma used to make them. You can also prepare some of the fabulous recipes made by your friends' grandmas.

Retail $21.95 7" x 10"
208 pages 10 colour photographs
ISBN 1-894022-86-6 perfect bound

201 MORE Fat-burning Recipes

by Cathi Graham

Featured on major radio and TV talk shows across Canada and the US, Cathi Graham's success story is inspirational. She lost 186 pounds over 20 years ago and has kept it off. Her second book of fat-burning recipes is filled with satisfying fibre-rich recipes that help raise the metabolism. Chicken with Prawns, Mango and orange salad, Pasta Alfredo Primavera, Lasagne, Sour Cream Coffee Cake – do these sound like diet recipes? No! and they don't taste diet; they taste fabulous.

Retail $19.95 5¾" x 8½"
220 pages 7 colour photographs
ISBN 1-897010-16-8 perfect bound

Grandma's Soups & Salads with Biscuits & Breads

by Irene Hrechuk and Verna Zasada

Over 100 superb soups and stews range from elegant chilled to hearty vegetable, seafood and meat. Over 70 fabulous salads include fruit, grains, pasta, vegetable and tossed salads. There are also over 25 satisfying yeast and quick breads. Outstanding variation suggestions effectively double the number of soup, salad and bread recipes. These are family-style recipes – grandma's comfort food.

Retail $21.95 7" x 10"
208 pages 10 colour photographs
ISBN 1-897010-02-8 perfect bound

Grandma's Best – Traditional Treats – over 200,000 sold in series

by Irene Hrechuk and Verna Zasada

Grandma's Best and *Grandma's Touch* represent the rich multicultural aspect of Canadian life and include treasured family recipes from many cultural groups. A special children's section has recipes that children love and love to make. This satisfying collection of grandma's favorite recipes will please everyone from grandkids to grandads. Here are the satisfying, comforting aromas and flavors that you remember from Grandma's kitchen.

Retail $21.95 7" x 10"
208 pages 10 colour photographs
ISBN 1-894022-66-1 perfect bound

Grandma's Touch – A Canadian Classic – over 200,000 sold in series

by Irene Hrechuk and Verna Zasada

Enjoy your special childhood favorites as Grandma used to make them, updated for today's busy, health-conscious cooks. Enjoy your favorite comfort food from your British, Chinese, French, German, Italian, Irish, Mexican, Russian, Scandinavian and Ukrainian grandmothers. These recipes, using readily available ingredients, are economical, easy to prepare and will delight beginner and experienced cooks.

Retail $21.95 7" x 10"
208 pages 10 colour photographs
ISBN 1-895292-62-9 perfect bound

CREATE YOUR OWN COOKBOOKS

My Holiday Recipes & Traditions

ISBN 1-894022-55-6

Recipes By Me & Other Special People

ISBN 1-894022-44-0

My College Survival Recipes

ISBN 1-894022-93-9

***Create Your Own Cookbooks* – each includes a roasting chart, herb and spice chart, ingredient substitutions, ingredient equivalent measures, metric conversion tables, kitchen tips and household hints.**

Each *Create Your Own Cookbook* retails for $12.95, 6" x 9", has 144 pages with illustrations throughout and lay-flat coil binding.